T0248106

GATHER

GATHER

100+ SEASONAL RECIPES THAT BRING PEOPLE TOGETHER

CHRIS VIAUD

Photographs by **PHIL VIAUD**

CIDER MILL PRESS

BOOK PUBLISHERS

Contents

Introduction

My journey as a chef began very early—as a toddler, helping Mom out in the kitchen. One of my earliest recollections is sitting on the floor with a mortar and pestle—or pilon, as it is known in Haitian Creole—and grinding herbs and spices for what I can only assume is the Haitian spice blend known as epis, a fundamental preparation in that cuisine, and in my own cooking.

At the time, I never would have imagined that the basic prep work I assisted my mother with—grinding aromatics, cutting up vegetables for soups and stews—would have such a large impact on my life. I was almost certainly just trying to spend more time with her, expressing my love by giving attention to the things she gave attention to. But, looking back from where I now stand, I know that in some way those early experiences shaped my decision to pursue a career in the culinary arts.

As a teenager, I frequently found myself watching cooking shows and flipping through cookbooks, activities that alerted me to the presence of an outsized love for food. My enthusiasm made it impossible to deny: I wanted to become a chef—a profession not exactly in line with the expectations in Haitian immigrant households, where it is accepted that education will lead one down a far more defined path to success, such as engineering, law, or the medical profession. Fortunately, my parents, though unfamiliar with the food service industry, supported my decision, and eventually I decided that Johnson & Wales University in Providence, Rhode Island, was the

place I wanted to be. I spent 4 years there, pursuing a bachelor's degree in Culinary Arts and Food Service Management, and picking up everything I could from my instructors, my peers, and the chefs I worked alongside. The more I learned, the greater my passion became, and though I could see how much further there was to go, I was undeterred. I could see that the path I'd set upon so many years ago was the correct one, and my confidence seemed to grow with the creation of each new dish, a feeling that carried me past any and all difficulties.

Still, as I worked my way up through the restaurant industry, I felt like something was missing. Like any chef, I enjoy working with quality ingredients. But eventually, I found that they alone were not enough to articulate what was inside of me. I wanted to create dishes that made them sing, of course. But I also wanted those dishes to have meaning, to do something more than simply satisfy a hungry guest. I wanted them to tell stories—mine, and those belonging to the people I knew and loved.

Attempting to communicate my own story through food was still a long way off, however, as I came up at a time when there were strictly defined parameters regarding the cuisines worthy of a chef's talents—with classical French and Italian cooking leading the way. I spent 3 formative years working in a fine-dining restaurant in Boston, where I learned the discipline required to succeed in a professional kitchen, and how to manage one's time. I then shifted to a more corporate setting where I learned a lot about the operations side of running a restaurant. That job led to my first executive chef position, where I was able to build a kitchen and a team from scratch.

After leaving that job, I worked in high-end, farm-to-table catering, a position that eventually turned into an opportunity to open my first restaurant, Greenleaf. A bakery, Culture, quickly followed. Located in southern New Hampshire, I was determined to use both establishments to alert people in the area as to what food could be.

Thankfully, those efforts did not go unnoticed. In 2021, I was invited to compete on Bravo's *Top Chef*, an experience that marked a major shift in my evolution as a chef, and provided much of the inspiration for this cookbook. During that competition, I found myself surrounded by enormously talented chefs who had embraced the food of their own cultural heritages. Working with them showed me that I have potential to be a part of the transformation currently underway in the industry, where more and more of the world's cuisines are gaining exposure and esteem. Through my time there, I gained a greater appreciation for the Haitian foods that shaped my earliest experiences in the kitchen, and developed a much deeper respect for the flavors present within them.

From there, the concept for my next restaurant, Ansanm, started to take shape. The Haitian Creole word for "together," it expressed my desire to find ways to share those flavors and dishes that had come back to life for me thanks to my time at *Top Chef*, and capitalize on food's unique ability to communicate with complete strangers and unite people of various backgrounds.

It is that bringing people together around a table, opening people up to new experiences and different cultures, and creating lasting memories that guided this cookbook. It is a mélange of all my experiences, with dishes tailored to the gatherings that give shape to each season. It is a blend of everything I love about food—the traditional dishes of my family, the elevated ones that my training and development have influenced, and those recipes that have resulted from my attempts to combine the two.

As you no doubt can feel from this brief introduction, food is very much a family affair for me. That has carried over to this book—not just in terms of the dishes that have been included, but also in the photographs, which are the handiwork of my incredibly talented brother, Phil. Getting to work together on *Gather*, with each of us having the opportunity to express ourselves via the medium we have dedicated ourselves to, is a dream come true.

I have been beyond fortunate in my life as a chef, and while this book is yet another milestone, I know it is far from the end. Even while working nonstop to finish it and run my restaurants, I added another establishment to my company, Northern Comfort Hospitality Group, taking over ownership of an established contemporary American restaurant known as Pavilion in Wolfeboro, New Hampshire. My focus there will be to provide space for passionate individuals to find their own voices, to continue to share those things that I love, and, of course, to create moments where people from all walks of life can come together, listen to one another, and celebrate each other.

Spring

The numbing air of winter has finally departed. The world rushes back to life, and with that comes local produce like asparagus, baby potatoes, and fresh peas. You can once again venture outside without hesitation, and revel in the glory laid before you. The exuberance all of this can't help but have an impact on what comes out of your kitchen, calling for light, fresh, and vibrant preparations that will supply endless opportunities to celebrate.

Yield: 3 Cups
Active Time: 10 Minutes
Total Time: 10 Minutes

Creamy, smoky, slightly sweet, and with just a bit of bite, this dip is the appetizer you want on that first spring day where summer feels close, when all you want to do is sit outside with friends and family. It's as good with crackers or chips as it is with crudités.

Spring Onion Dip

½ lb. cream cheese, softened

½ cup sour cream, at room temperature

1 tablespoon honey

1½ teaspoons kosher salt

¼ cup mayonnaise

1½ teaspoons smoked paprika

½ cup sliced spring onions

1 Place the cream cheese in the work bowl of a stand mixer fitted with the whisk attachment and whip on high until it is light and fluffy.

2 Add the remaining ingredients and whip until well combined.

3 Taste the dip, adjust the seasoning as necessary, and serve immediately.

Yield: 2 Servings
Active Time: 10 Minutes
Total Time: 15 Minutes

I've always loved cabbage, and when I first learned about bok choy, that love reached new levels, as I knew I had discovered an extremely versatile vegetable. Its crunchy stalk, leafy greens, and subtle grassy, peppery flavor allow me to utilize a number of techniques in preparing it, but I find that blanching it first helps bring out its vibrant green color.

Baby Bok Choy
with Salsa Macha

Salt and pepper, to taste

4 baby bok choy, trimmed and halved lengthwise

2 tablespoons extra-virgin olive oil

2 cups oyster mushrooms, sliced

1 red bell pepper, stem and seeds removed, sliced

1 small onion, sliced

½ cup Salsa Macha (see page 73)

1 Bring water to a boil in a large saucepan and prepare an ice bath. Add salt until the water tastes like sea water. Add the bok choy and cook until it is just tender, about 2 minutes. Drain the bok choy, plunge it into the ice bath, and drain again. Transfer the bok choy to a paper towel–lined plate and let it dry.

2 Place the olive oil in a large skillet and warm it over medium heat. Add the mushrooms, season them with salt and pepper, and cook, stirring occasionally, until they are browned, 10 to 12 minutes.

3 Add the peppers and onion and cook, stirring occasionally, until they are tender, about 8 minutes.

4 Stir in the bok choy and cook until it is warmed through. Transfer the vegetables to a serving dish, drizzle the Salsa Macha over the top, and serve.

Yield: 2 Servings
Active Time: 10 Minutes
Total Time: 20 Minutes

When you leave the skin on a piece of salmon and cook it just right, the contrast between the crispy skin and the creamy flesh of the fish is divine. Chermoula, a North African condiment, is great with seafood, and exceptional with salmon prepared in this manner.

Crispy Salmon
with Red Chermoula

1 tablespoon canola oil

1 lb. skin-on salmon fillets, cut into 4-oz. pieces

Salt and pepper, to taste

2 tablespoons unsalted butter

3 sprigs of fresh thyme

2 garlic cloves, crushed

½ lemon

Red Chermoula Sauce (see page 66)

Fresh herbs, finely chopped, for garnish

1 Preheat the oven to 450°F. Place the canola oil in a large cast-iron skillet and warm it over medium-high heat. Season the salmon with salt and pepper and carefully place it in the pan, skin side down. Place the pan in the oven and roast it for 3 to 4 minutes, depending on the thickness of the pieces of salmon.

2 Remove the pan from the oven and add the butter, thyme, and garlic. Baste the salmon with the butter until its internal temperature is 135°F.

3 Squeeze the juice of the lemon into the pan and baste the salmon a few more times.

4 Transfer the salmon to a paper towel–lined plate to drain briefly.

5 Place the salmon on the serving plates, drizzle the chermoula over the top, garnish with fresh herbs, and serve.

Minimal ingredients are required to make this light and airy cake. But that humble construction will not be evident to your guests, as the pearly white crumb and beautifully burnished exterior make for a showstopping dessert.

Angel Food Cake
with Passion Fruit Sauce

1½ cups sugar

1 cup cake flour

¼ teaspoon fine sea salt

12 egg whites

1½ teaspoons cream of tartar

1½ teaspoons pure vanilla extract

Passion Fruit Sauce (see page 20)

Whipped cream, for garnish

Orange slices, for garnish

1 Preheat the oven to 325°F. Place the sugar in a food processor and blitz until the sugar is fine, about 2 minutes. Remove 1 cup of sugar and set it aside.

2 Add the flour and salt to the work bowl of the food processor and pulse to combine.

3 Place the egg whites, cream of tartar, vanilla, and reserved sugar in the work bowl of a stand mixer fitted with the whisk attachment. Whip on high until the meringue holds soft peaks.

4 Sift the flour mixture over the meringue and fold to incorporate it.

5 Pour the batter into a 10-cup Bundt pan that has not been greased and place it in the oven.

6 Bake the cake until a cake tester inserted into its center comes out clean, about 40 minutes.

7 Remove the cake from the oven, invert the pan on a wire rack, and let the cake cool for 1 hour before removing it from the pan.

8 Garnish the cake with whipped cream and orange slices and top each portion with some of the sauce.

Yield: 1½ Cups
Active Time: 20 Minutes
Total Time: 1 Hour

The beguiling sour flavor of passion fruit is severely underutilized. This silky sauce, which will inevitably find its way into a number of other preparations, helps remedy that.

Passion Fruit Sauce

2 cups orange juice

3 tablespoons sugar

⅛ teaspoon fine sea salt

2 passion fruits

1 Place the orange juice, sugar, and salt in a small saucepan and bring to a boil. Cook until it has reduced by half.

2 Cut the passion fruits in half and scoop the pulp and seeds into the pan. Stir to combine and cook for 2 minutes.

3 Taste, adjust the seasoning as necessary, and remove the pan from heat. Let the sauce cool completely before serving.

Encasing toasted slivers of almond in buttery toffee makes for a light yet decadent treat that can be enjoyed on its own, or used as a topping to lift other desserts.

Almond Brittle

½ cup unsalted butter

2½ cups slivered almonds

2 cups sugar

½ cup water

2 teaspoons kosher salt

1 teaspoon baking soda

1 Line a baking sheet with parchment paper.

2 Place the butter in a small saucepan and melt it over medium-low heat. Add the almonds and cook, stirring occasionally, until they become fragrant, about 5 minutes.

3 Place the sugar, water, and salt in a medium saucepan and bring to a boil. Cook, swirling the pan occasionally, until the mixture is 310°F.

4 Stir in the almonds and butter, being careful as the syrup may splatter.

5 Remove the pan from heat, add the baking soda, and quickly stir to incorporate it.

6 Spread the mixture over the baking sheet, smoothing the top with a rubber spatula.

7 Let the almond brittle cool completely until breaking it up into smaller pieces and serving.

A sweet-and-sour cocktail made for those days where the bright spring sun is calling you and your loved ones outdoors. For the ginger liqueur, either Barrow's or Domaine de Canton are your best bets.

Let the Sun Shine

1½ oz. vodka

½ oz. ginger liqueur

1½ oz. kumquat syrup

½ oz. fresh lime juice

2 oz. passion fruit puree

1 Candied Kumquat (see page 25), for garnish

1 Place all of the ingredients, except for the Candied Kumquat, in a cocktail shaker, fill it halfway with ice, and shake vigorously for 10 seconds.

2 Strain over ice into a highball glass, garnish with a Candied Kumquat, and enjoy.

Yield: 1 Cup
Active Time: 30 Minutes
Total Time: 9 Hours

Although they can hard to come by, whenever I come across these fun little citrus fruits I try to find a way to incorporate them into dishes or beverages that I am working on. A few things to know for the unfamiliar—kumquats have the flavor of an orange, the tartness of a lemon, and the whole fruit is edible.

Candied Kumquats

½ cup water

1 cup sugar

1 cup halved kumquats, seeds removed

1 Place the water and sugar in a small saucepan and bring to a boil, stirring to dissolve the sugar.

2 Add the kumquats and cook on very low heat for about 15 minutes.

3 Strain the kumquats, reserving the syrup for the preparation of the Let the Sun Shine cocktail on page 23.

4 Place the kumquats on a dehydrator tray or baking sheet. Set a dehydrator or oven to 130°F (if the oven can go that low), place the kumquats in it, and dehydrate for 8 hours. Use immediately or store them in an airtight container.

Yield: 4 to 6 Servings
Active Time: 20 Minutes
Total Time: 45 Minutes

Ginger's spice plays well with the natural sweetness of the carrots, and this pair is perfect for those chilly days that are inevitable in early spring. The heavy cream and crème fraîche will make this a much richer and creamier soup, but they are not necessary if you are looking for a healthier option.

Carrot & Ginger Bisque

2 tablespoons unsalted butter

1 large onion, sliced

5 garlic cloves, sliced

2 oz. fresh ginger, peeled and sliced

2 lbs. carrots, peeled and chopped

Salt and pepper, to taste

6 cups Roasted Chicken Stock (see page 214)

1 cup heavy cream

1 cup crème fraîche

Toasted nuts, for garnish

Herb Oil (see page 108), for garnish

1 Place the butter in a medium saucepan and melt it over medium heat. Add the onion, garlic, and ginger and cook, stirring frequently, until they have softened, about 5 minutes.

2 Add the carrots, season with salt and pepper, and add the stock. Bring the soup to a boil, reduce the heat, and let the soup simmer until the carrots are tender, about 15 minutes.

3 Add the heavy cream and half of the crème fraîche and gently simmer the soup for 10 minutes.

4 Strain the soup, reserving the liquid. Transfer the solids to a blender and puree until smooth, using the reserved liquid to reach the desired consistency. Taste the soup and adjust the seasoning as necessary.

5 Pour the soup into warmed bowls, garnish each portion with toasted nuts, Herb Oil, and the remaining crème fraîche, and serve.

Yield: 2 to 4 Servings
Active Time: 20 Minutes
Total Time: 20 Minutes

Getting a nice hard sear on the vegetables that belong to the brassica family—broccoli, Brussels sprouts, cabbage, kale, and cauliflower to name a few—brings out the unique sweetness that they have to offer. There are many ways you can achieve this sear: in a very hot pan, which is the option suggested here, in an oven set at a high temperature, or on a grill.

Charred Broccoli
with Lemon & Parmesan Vinaigrette

For the Broccoli

Salt and pepper, to taste

2 crowns of broccoli, quartered

3 tablespoons canola oil

½ cup Pickled Red Onion (see page 120), for garnish

½ cup toasted pine nuts, for garnish

For the Vinaigrette

1 egg yolk

¼ cup grated Parmesan cheese

2 tablespoons fresh lemon juice

1 teaspoon Dijon mustard

1 cup canola oil

1 To begin preparations for the broccoli, bring water to a boil in a large saucepan and prepare an ice bath. Add salt until the water tastes like sea water (about 3 tablespoons of salt). Add the broccoli and cook for 1 minute. Remove the broccoli with a strainer and plunge it into the ice bath. Drain the broccoli and let it dry on a paper towel–lined plate.

2 To prepare the vinaigrette, place all of the ingredients, except for the canola oil, in a small bowl and stir to combine. While whisking continually, slowly stream in the canola oil until it has emulsified. Taste, adjust the seasoning as necessary, and set the vinaigrette aside.

3 Place the canola oil in a large skillet and warm it over high heat. Lightly season the broccoli with salt and pepper and place it in the pan, taking care not to crowd the pan. Sear the broccoli until it is lightly charred on both sides.

4 Spread the vinaigrette over a serving dish, arrange the broccoli on top, garnish with the pickled onions and toasted pine nuts, and serve.

Yield: 1½ Cups
Active Time: 10 Minutes
Total Time: 10 Minutes

The mixture of herbs associated with green goddess is typically used in a salad dressing, but by cutting back a bit on the acid and oil, you can ramp up the freshness factor and create a pesto that is far more versatile, capable of being used on sandwiches, pastas, meat dishes, and more.

Green Goddess Pesto

¼ cup chopped celery leaves

½ cup chopped fresh parsley

2 tablespoons chopped fresh tarragon

½ cup sliced fresh chives

¾ cup sunflower seeds, toasted

2 teaspoons fine sea salt

1 teaspoon black pepper

1 teaspoon fresh lemon juice

Zest of 1 lemon

¾ cup canola oil

¼ cup extra-virgin olive oil

1 Place all of the ingredients, except for the oils, in a food processor and blitz to combine.

2 With the food processor running, slowly stream in the oils until they have emulsified.

3 Taste the pesto, adjust the seasoning as necessary, and either use immediately or store it in the refrigerator.

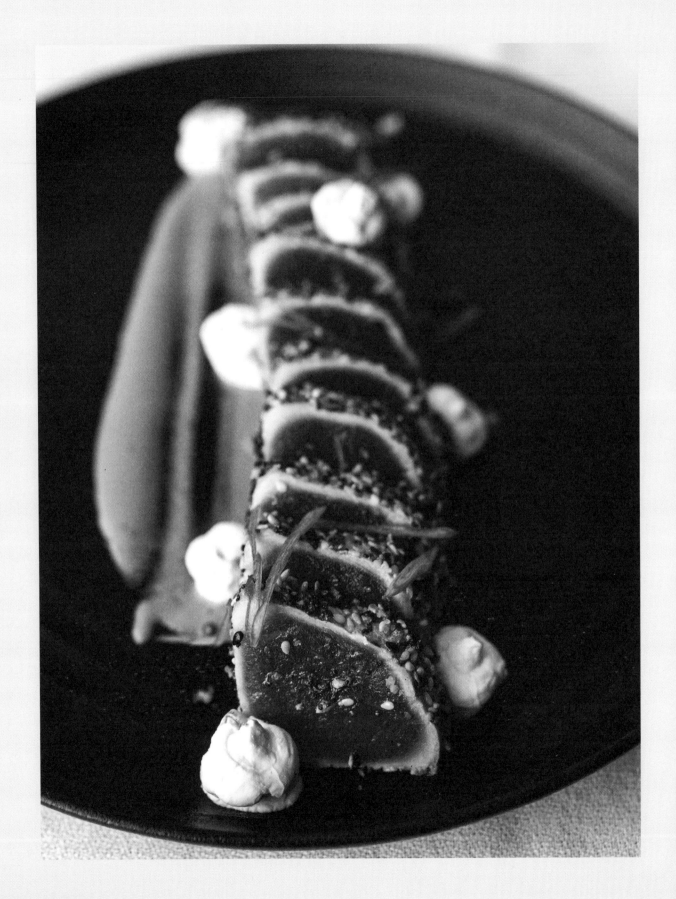

Yield: 2 Servings
Active Time: 20 Minutes
Total Time: 30 Minutes

I'm a big believer that food shouldn't just be flavorful, it should also be fun—particularly when you're hosting friends and family. In keeping with that, I deconstructed one of my favorite breakfasts—an everything bagel with cream cheese—and turned it into a seafood dish. The key to working with tuna is getting the sear just right and using a very sharp knife to cut it—do both, and the presentation will be unparalleled.

Everything Spice Tuna
with Scallion Cream Cheese

For the Scallion Puree

Salt, to taste

½ lb. scallions, trimmed

1 garlic clove, sliced

1 lemon peel

¼ cup canola oil

For the Tuna

1 tablespoon onion flakes

¾ tablespoon garlic flakes

1½ teaspoons white sesame seeds

1½ teaspoons black sesame seeds

1½ teaspoons poppy seeds

½ lb. tuna steaks

Salt and white pepper, to taste

2 tablespoons canola oil

Scallion Cream Cheese (see page 34), for garnish

1 To begin preparations for the scallion puree, bring water to a boil in a medium saucepan and prepare an ice bath. Add salt and the scallions, garlic, and lemon peel and cook for 2 minutes. Remove the mixture with a strainer and plunge it into the ice bath. Drain the mixture and squeeze it to remove excess moisture.

2 Place the mixture in a blender and puree until smooth. With the blender running, slowly stream in the canola oil until it has emulsified. Taste the puree, adjust the seasoning as necessary, and set the puree aside.

3 To begin preparations for the tuna, place the garlic flakes, onion flakes, sesame seeds, and poppy seeds on a plate and stir to combine.

4 Season the tuna with salt and white pepper and roll it in the seed mixture.

5 Place the canola oil in a large cast-iron skillet and warm it over high heat. Add the tuna and sear it for just 10 seconds on each side.

6 Remove the tuna from the pan and slice it.

7 To serve, spread the scallion puree over the plates, arrange some tuna beside it, and top with dollops of the Scallion Cream Cheese.

Yield: ¾ Cup
Active Time: 5 Minutes
Total Time: 5 Minutes

Infusing cream cheese with the subtle flavor of scallions makes for a surprisingly versatile spread, one that is as comfortable beside a beautiful piece of fish as it is on a slice of toasted bread.

Scallion Cream Cheese

½ cup cream cheese, softened

2 tablespoons minced scallions

½ teaspoon kosher salt

¼ teaspoon white pepper

1 teaspoon lemon zest

1 Place all of the ingredients in a bowl and stir to combine.

2 Use the cream cheese immediately or store it in the refrigerator.

Yield: 4 Servings
Active Time: 30 Minutes
Total Time: 6 Hours

Fried Chicken Sandwich

For the Chicken

2 cups buttermilk

1½ teaspoons sazon

1 tablespoon Epis
(see page 104)

1 tablespoon Pikliz brine
(see page 63)

1 tablespoon adobo seasoning

4 boneless chicken thighs

For the Breading

2 cups all-purpose flour

1 teaspoon black pepper

1 teaspoon adobo seasoning

1 teaspoon sazon

2 teaspoons garlic powder

Canola oil, as needed

Salt, to taste

4 Adobo Brioche Buns
(see page 157), split open

4 slices of cheddar

8 slices of bacon, cooked

Epis Mayonnaise (see page 38)

Pikliz

When I was opening up my Haitian restaurant in New Hampshire, one big challenge was finding ways to present the Haitian flavors I loved to people who were unfamiliar with them while still being approachable. This sandwich proved to be the perfect vehicle, as fried chicken, an herbaceous sauce, and a spicy slaw gets people on board pretty quickly.

1 To begin preparations for the chicken, place all of the ingredients, except for the chicken, in a mixing bowl and stir to combine. Add the chicken, stir until it is coated, and let the chicken marinate in the refrigerator for 4 to 6 hours.

2 To prepare the breading, place all of the ingredients in a large baking pan and stir to combine.

3 Remove the chicken from the marinade and dredge it in the breading until evenly coated.

4 Add canola oil to a Dutch oven until it is about 2 inches deep and warm it to 325°F.

5 Gently slip the chicken into the hot oil and cook until it is crispy and the interior temperature is 165°F. Do your best to maintain the oil's temperature as the chicken cooks, working in batches if necessary.

6 Transfer the fried chicken to a paper towel–lined plate to drain and season it with salt.

7 Assemble the sandwiches with the fried chicken, brioche buns, cheddar, bacon, Epis Mayonnaise, and Pikliz.

Salsa Macha, see page 73

Yield: 1 Cup
Active Time: 5 Minutes
Total Time: 5 Minutes

Epis is a Haitian spice blend and one of my culinary touch-stones. It is also a malleable flavoring agent, able to facilitate a conversation between Haiti and dishes from other cuisines with ease.

Epis Mayonnaise

1 tablespoon Epis (see page 104)

1 cup mayonnaise

1 teaspoon fresh lime juice

1 tablespoon minced scallion

1 tablespoon chopped fresh parsley

1 Place all of the ingredients in a bowl and stir to combine.

2 Use the mayonnaise immediately or store it in the refrigerator.

Yield: 2½ Cups
Active Time: 10 Minutes
Total Time: 1 Hour

Don't be deceived by the name—there is nothing simple about the role this plays in crafting cocktails, as it is essential to balance flavors and provide a drink with the proper mouthfeel.

Simple Syrup

1 cup water

2 cups sugar

1 Place water in a small saucepan and bring to a boil.

2 Add the sugar and stir until the sugar has dissolved.

3 Remove the pan from heat and let the simple syrup cool completely before using or storing in the refrigerator.

When the weather gets warm and a family gathering is on the schedule, everyone knows that this punch will be on hand. You can use any rum, but I like the smooth flavor of Haitian rum here. Also, while this recipe is for an individual serving, you can easily make a large batch by maintaining the ratios and multiplying by the number of servings you'd like.

Rum Punch

2 oz. Barbancourt 5-Star rum

1½ oz. orange juice

1½ oz. pineapple juice

1½ oz. fresh lime juice

1 tablespoon grenadine

1 tablespoon Simple Syrup
(see page 39)

1 lime wheel, for garnish

1 maraschino cherry,
for garnish

1 Fill a highball glass with ice and set it aside.

2 Place all of the ingredients, except for the garnishes, in a cocktail shaker, fill it halfway with ice, and shake vigorously for 15 seconds.

3 Strain the punch over the ice, garnish with the lime wheel and cherry, and enjoy.

Yield: 1 Cake

Active Time: 15 Minutes

Total Time: 1 Hour and 30 Minutes

Seemingly every chef has a carrot cake recipe in their portfolio, and this one is actually an adaptation of a recipe I conceived for an art show, where I had to pull inspiration from a particular piece. If you're looking to make this cake a little more eye-catching, top it with some of the Almond Brittle (see page 21).

Carrot Cake

½ cup unsalted butter

1 cup sugar

2 eggs

1¾ cups plus 2 tablespoons all-purpose flour

1 teaspoon cinnamon

1 teaspoon freshly grated nutmeg

2 teaspoon baking powder

1 teaspoon fine sea salt

2 cups grated carrots

Toasted Almond Buttercream (see page 46)

1 Place the butter in a large skillet and melt it over medium heat. Cook the butter until it starts to brown and give off a nutty aroma. Remove the pan from heat and let the brown butter cool completely.

2 Preheat the oven to 325°F.

3 Place the sugar and eggs in the work bowl of a stand mixer fitted with the paddle attachment and beat on low until the mixture is pale and fluffy.

4 In a separate bowl, combine the flour, cinnamon, nutmeg, baking powder, and salt. Set the mixture aside.

5 Add the brown butter and carrots to the work bowl and beat to incorporate. Add the dry mixture and beat until the mixture just comes together as a batter.

6 Coat a 9 x 5-inch loaf pan with nonstick cooking spray and pour the batter into it. Tap the pan on the counter a few times to remove any air bubbles and place it in the oven.

7 Bake until a cake tester inserted into the center of the cake comes out clean, 40 to 45 minutes. Remove the cake from the oven and let it cool completely.

8 Frost the cake with the buttercream, slice, and serve.

Infusing a rich buttercream with the nutty, vanilla-inclined flavor of toasted almonds makes for an exceptional frosting, and adds a contrasting texture that will prove memorable atop a moist, soft cake.

Toasted Almond Buttercream

1 cup slivered almonds

2 cups cream cheese, softened

½ cup unsalted butter, softened

½ cup confectioners' sugar

1 teaspoon fine sea salt

1 Preheat the oven to 350°F. Place the almonds on a baking sheet and place them in the oven. Toast the almonds until they are fragrant and golden brown, about 6 minutes. Remove the toasted almonds from the oven.

2 Place the remaining ingredients in the work bowl of a stand mixer fitted with the paddle attachment and beat on low to combine.

3 Add the toasted almonds, beat to combine, and raise the speed to high. Beat until the frosting is fluffy.

4 Use the frosting immediately or store it in the refrigerator.

One of the best developments in modern cooking is the insistence that salads can be bright and stand up, flavor- and imagination-wise, to the rest of the meal. As you'll see in other instances in the book, cranberry and orange is one of those pairings that works really well, and combining it with crisp fresh vegetables and sweet Candied Pecans makes for a perfect start to a memorable meal.

Mixed Greens Salad
with Cranberry & Orange Vinaigrette

For the Vinaigrette

2 tablespoons apple cider vinegar

1 tablespoon honey

1½ teaspoons kosher salt

Zest of 1 orange

¼ cup fresh orange juice

1½ teaspoon Dijon mustard

½ cup fresh cranberries

½ cup canola oil

For the Salad

½ lb. mixed greens

½ cup shaved radishes

½ cup shaved carrots

½ cup Candied Pecans (see page 162)

½ red onion, sliced

1 Asian pear, cored and sliced

1 To prepare the vinaigrette, place all of the ingredients, except for the canola oil, in a blender and puree on low until combined. Raise the speed to medium and slowly stream in the canola oil until it has emulsified. Taste, adjust the seasoning as necessary, and set the vinaigrette aside.

2 To prepare the salad, place all of the ingredients in a salad bowl and toss to combine. Add some of the vinaigrette, toss to combine, and serve the salad with the remaining vinaigrette alongside.

Yield: 2 Servings
Active Time: 15 Minutes
Total Time: 30 Minutes

I like to make this dish when something quick and easy is all the day will allow for, as I know the preparation doesn't require much work, and the outcome is assured to be delicious.

Herb-Crusted Cod
with Caper Cream

1 lb. cod loin, cut into 4 pieces

1½ cups panko

1 tablespoon chopped fresh parsley, plus more for garnish

1 tablespoon chopped fresh chives, plus more for garnish

1 tablespoon chopped fresh basil, plus more for garnish

Salt and pepper, to taste

2 tablespoons canola oil

Caper Cream
(see opposite page)

Lemon wedges, for serving

1 Preheat the oven to 400°F. Pat the cod dry with paper towels. Place the panko and fresh herbs in a food processor, season with salt and pepper, and pulse to combine. Set the mixture aside.

2 Place the canola oil in a large cast-iron skillet and warm it over high heat. Season the cod with salt and pepper and dredge one side in the panko mixture. Place it in the pan, panko topping facing up, reduce the heat to medium, and cook until the edges of the cod start to brown.

3 Transfer the cod to the oven and roast until it is cooked through and the topping is golden brown, 6 to 8 minutes.

4 Remove the pan from the oven. Using a fish spatula, carefully remove the fish from the pan and place it in a serving dish.

5 Spoon the Caper Cream into the dish, garnish with fresh herbs, and serve with lemon wedges.

Yield: 1½ Cups
Active Time: 15 Minutes
Total Time: 40 Minutes

Here, we use a rich, creamy sauce to build a bridge between the bright and bold citrus and the briny pop of the capers.

Caper Cream

2 tablespoons unsalted butter

2 tablespoons diced shallot

2 garlic cloves, minced

2 tablespoons capers

2 tablespoons white wine

1 cup heavy cream

1 tablespoon fresh lemon juice

Salt, to taste

1 Place the butter in a small saucepan and melt it over medium heat. Add the shallot and garlic and cook, stirring continually, for 1 minute. Add the capers and wine and cook until the wine has evaporated.

2 Add the cream and cook, stirring continually, until it has reduced by half.

3 Add the lemon juice, taste, and season with salt. Remove the pan from heat and let the caper cream cool before using.

Herb-Crusted Cod with Caper Cream, see page 50

Yield: 2 Sheets
Active Time: 10 Minutes
Total Time: 40 Minutes

This dough is a hybrid between piecrust dough and puff pastry, making it a great fit for savory or sweet applications, from quiche and tarts to handpies and decadent pastries.

Quick Pastry Dough

2 cups all-purpose flour, plus more as needed

1 teaspoon fine sea salt

1¼ cups unsalted butter, cubed

½ cup cold water

1 Place the flour and salt in a food processor and pulse to combine.

2 Add the butter and pulse twice. Use a small rubber spatula to get the flour from the bottom of the work bowl to come up. Pulse the mixture twice more.

3 Add the water and pulse twice. Use a small rubber spatula to get the flour from the bottom of the work bowl to come up. Pulse the mixture twice more.

4 Place the dough on a flour-dusted work surface and press it into a rough rectangle. Flour the dough and press down on it with a rolling pin—you don't want to roll it yet—to flatten the dough.

5 Make sure that the work surface and dough are generously dusted with flour. Roll the dough into an 18-inch square and cut it in half.

6 Roll out one piece into a 12 x 18–inch rectangle. Working from a long side, fold the dough over itself as you would a letter. Working from a short side, roll the dough into a tight log and press down on it with your hands until it is a rough square. Repeat with the other piece of dough.

7 Cover the puff pastry with plastic wrap and chill it in the refrigerator for 30 minutes before using.

Yield: 1 Drink
Active Time: 5 Minutes
Total Time: 5 Minutes

The first sip of this cocktail will wow your palate, moving quickly from the bright and fresh strawberry to the creamy coconut and subtle bite from the shrub.

Island Dream

2 strawberries, plus 1 for garnish

4 fresh basil leaves, plus more for garnish

1 lime wedge

2 oz. vodka

1¼ oz. Strawberry Shrub (see page 58)

¼ oz. coconut milk

¼ oz. fresh lime juice

1 Fill a glass with ice and set it aside.

2 Place the strawberries, basil, and lime wedge in a cocktail shaker and muddle.

3 Add the remaining ingredients, fill the shaker halfway with ice, and shake vigorously for 15 seconds.

4 Strain the cocktail over ice, garnish with an additional strawberry and basil, and enjoy.

You can use any fruit to make a shrub, combining it with equal amounts of sugar and vinegar. Shrubs are a great way to cut down on waste, and will really enhance your beverage game, as their brightness will even invigorate a drink as simple as club soda and ice.

Strawberry Shrub

½ cup hulled and sliced strawberries

½ cup sugar

½ cup apple cider vinegar

1 Place all of the ingredients in a small saucepan and bring the mixture to a simmer over medium-high heat, stirring to dissolve the sugar.

2 Cook for 5 to 8 minutes and strain the shrub.

3 Let the shrub cool completely before using or storing in the refrigerator.

Yield: 2 to 4 Servings
Active Time: 10 Minutes
Total Time: 1 Hour and 30 Minutes

Pan-Seared Scallops
with Marinated Radishes & Pickled Kumquats

When given proper care and attention, scallops are a sweet and surprisingly decadent treat. To make sure you end up in the right place, you want to pat the scallops dry before searing and ensure that you do not crowd the pan with too many of them, as this will prevent the scallops from getting a nice, golden brown crust.

The marinated radishes can be made a day in advance, and it is recommended that you do, since their flavor and texture improve the longer they marinate.

2 watermelon radishes, trimmed and diced

½ cup extra-virgin olive oil

¼ cup honey

2 teaspoons rice vinegar

2 teaspoons soy sauce

1 teaspoon sesame oil

1 teaspoon grated fresh ginger

2 teaspoons minced shallot

1 lb. fresh scallops

Salt and white pepper, to taste

3 tablespoons canola oil

2 tablespoons unsalted butter

Pickled Kumquats (see page 62), for garnish

Scallions, chopped, for garnish

Black sesame seeds, toasted, for garnish

1 Place the radishes in a bowl. Place the olive oil, honey, vinegar, soy sauce, sesame oil, ginger, and shallot in a separate bowl and whisk to combine. Pour the mixture over the radishes and let them marinate for 45 minutes.

2 Pat the scallops dry with paper towels and season them with salt and white pepper. Place the canola oil in a large skillet and warm it over high heat.

3 Taking care not to crowd the pan, add the scallops and sear until golden brown on the bottom, 1 to 2 minutes.

4 Turn the scallops over, add the butter, and cook the scallops, frequently basting them with the butter, until their interior temperature is 125°F.

5 Transfer the scallops to a paper towel–lined plate and let them drain briefly.

6 Serve the scallops with the radishes and garnish with the Pickled Kumquats, scallions, and black sesame seeds.

Yield: 6 Servings
Active Time: 10 Minutes
Total Time: 1 Hour

Pickling kumquats adds a touch of acidity to their tropical sweetness, making them a great option for rounding out lighter dishes.

Pickled Kumquats

½ lb. kumquats, halved and seeded

2 cups rice vinegar

2 tablespoons sugar

½ teaspoon kosher salt

1 Place the kumquats in a mason jar.

2 Place the vinegar, sugar, and salt in a small saucepan and bring to a boil, stirring to dissolve the sugar and salt.

3 Pour the brine over the kumquats and let them cool completely before using or storing in the refrigerator.

Yield: 4 Cups
Active Time: 30 Minutes
Total Time: 2 to 3 Days

This spicy condiment is a classic Haitian preparation that I continually discover new uses for. It has the perfect amount of heat and refreshing citrus, and by brining the vegetables instead of pickling them, they remain crispy while having their flavor significantly enhanced.

Pikliz

¼ head of cabbage, sliced thin

1 large carrot, peeled and shredded

2 large shallots, sliced

¼ red bell pepper, sliced

¼ green bell pepper, sliced

¼ orange bell pepper, sliced

2 scotch bonnet or habanero chile peppers, stems and seeds removed, sliced

Juice of 1 lime

4 cups white vinegar

2 teaspoons kosher salt

1 Place the cabbage, carrot, shallots, and bell peppers in a large bowl.

2 Place the chile peppers, lime juice, and ¼ cup of the vinegar in a separate, microwave-safe bowl. Place the bowl in the microwave and microwave for 2 minutes, which will bring out all of the spice in the peppers. Remove the bowl from the microwave and let the mixture cool completely.

3 Pour the chile pepper mixture over the sliced vegetables and stir to combine. Add the remaining vinegar until the mixture is completely covered and then stir in the salt.

4 Cover the bowl with plastic wrap, place it in the refrigerator, and let the pikliz marinate for 48 to 72 hours before serving.

Pikliz, see page 63

Yield: 1 Cup
Active Time: 10 Minutes
Total Time: 10 Minutes

Chermoula, a North African sauce that is primarily used on seafood, has become a favorite spice blend of mine, as it is reminiscent of the flavors in Haitian cuisine that mean so much to me. Filled with herbs and spices, this sauce can be used as a marinade or brushed on meats or seafood while on the grill. And do not fret if preserved lemons are not available—just use the zest of 1 lemon.

Red Chermoula Sauce

Pinch saffron threads

¼ cup Harissa (see page 238)

½ cup extra-virgin olive oil

1 tablespoon chopped preserved lemons

2 teaspoons kosher salt

1 tablespoon smoked paprika

1 teaspoon cumin powder

2 teaspoons fresh lemon juice

2 tablespoons chopped fresh cilantro

1 tablespoon chopped fresh parsley

1 tablespoon sliced fresh chives

1 Using a mortar and pestle or food processor, combine all of the ingredients, except for the herbs, until the desired consistency has been achieved.

2 Add the herbs and stir until well combined.

3 Taste the sauce, adjust the seasoning as necessary, and use immediately or store it in the refrigerator.

Ricotta is by far one of the easier cheeses to make at home. That said, it will still impress guests, and it has the ability to elevate everything from a salad to toast.

Ricotta Cheese

8 cups whole milk

1 tablespoon kosher salt

½ cup fresh lemon juice or distilled white vinegar

1 Place the milk and salt in a small saucepan and warm it to 155°F.

2 Remove the pan from heat and add the lemon juice. Gently stir with a wooden spoon—you will begin to see the cheese curds form and separate from the whey.

3 Line a fine-mesh strainer with cheesecloth and place it over a bowl. Slowly pour the whey and cheese into the strainer and let the cheese drain.

4 Lift the cheesecloth containing the ricotta out of the strainer and use as desired.

Yield: 4 to 6 Servings
Active Time: 30 Minutes
Total Time: 2 Hours

Beets are one of those ingredients that many people are wary of, a feeling which likely stems from encountering them in some improperly prepared form. But, when cooked correctly, beets are sweet and delicious. And, contrary to what you think, their earthy character makes them a brilliant match for strawberries. To make the candied walnuts, follow the recipe on page 162 and substitute walnuts for the pecans.

Roasted Beet Salad

For the Salad

3 red beets

3 golden beets

3 pink baby beets

6 sprigs of fresh thyme

6 garlic cloves

3 tablespoons extra-virgin olive oil

3 tablespoons soy sauce

6 tablespoons water

2 oz. frisee

8 strawberries, halved

Salt and pepper, to taste

4 oz. goat cheese, crumbled

1 cup candied walnuts

For the Vinaigrette

2 tablespoons Champagne vinegar

1 teaspoon minced shallot

1 tablespoon honey

1 teaspoon Dijon mustard

½ teaspoon kosher salt

½ teaspoon black pepper

1 teaspoon chopped fresh oregano

¾ cup canola oil

1 Preheat the oven to 400°F. To begin preparations for the salad, group the beets according to color and place each group in a separate aluminum foil pouch. Divide the thyme, garlic, olive oil, soy sauce, and water between the pouches, seal them, and place them in a baking pan.

2 Place the pouches in the oven and roast the beets until a knife inserted into them passes easily to their centers, 45 minutes to 1 hour.

3 Remove the beets from the oven and let them cool.

4 When the beets are cool enough to handle, peel them and cut them into bite-size pieces. Place the beets in a bowl and let them cool completely.

5 Place the frisee and strawberries in a mixing bowl and toss to combine. Set the mixture aside.

6 To prepare the vinaigrette, place all of the ingredients, except for the canola oil, in a bowl and whisk to combine. While whisking continually, slowly stream in the canola oil until it has emulsified. Taste the vinaigrette and adjust the seasoning as necessary.

7 Add some vinaigrette to the bowl containing the beets, season with salt and pepper, and toss to combine. Place the beets in a serving bowl, layer the frisee mixture over them, and top with the goat cheese and candied walnuts. Serve with any remaining vinaigrette.

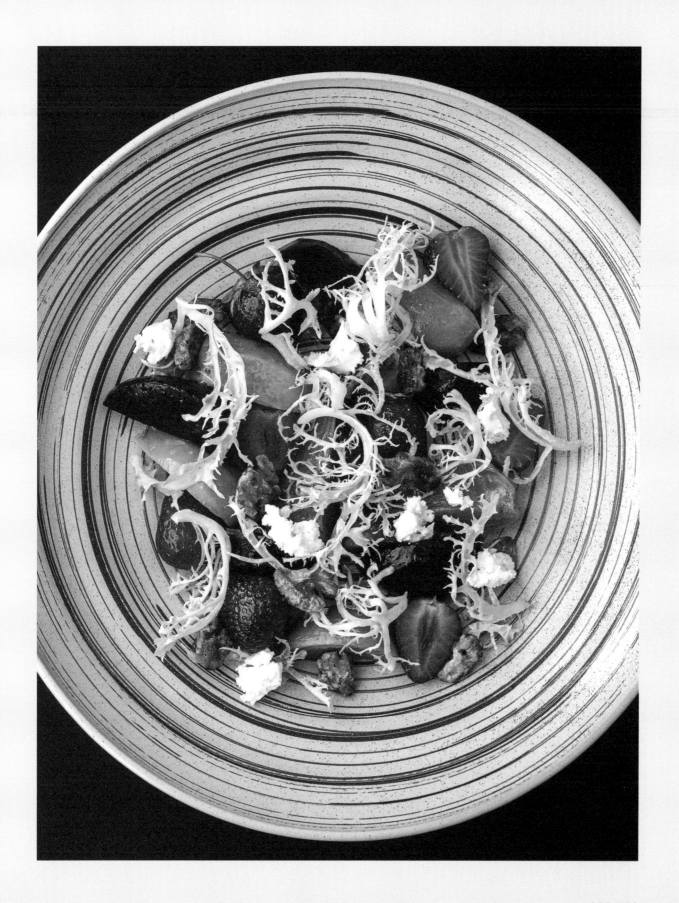

Yield: 2 Cups
Active Time: 5 Minutes
Total Time: 30 Minutes

When I first discovered this salsa I was so intrigued by its flavor and texture that I searched out as many ways to use it as possible. You'll likely embark on a similar search, thinking up new spots where its bold punch will come in handy.

Salsa Macha

1 cup raw unsalted peanuts

2 cups extra-virgin olive oil

5 garlic cloves, sliced

1 shallot, sliced

¼ cup sunflower seeds

½ teaspoon cumin seeds

½ teaspoon fennel seeds

1 tablespoon white sesame seeds

1 tablespoon black sesame seeds

1 tablespoon coriander seeds

2 ancho chile peppers, stems and seeds removed

2 guajillo chile peppers, stems and seeds removed

5 chiles de árbol, stems and seeds removed

1 teaspoon apple cider vinegar

Salt, to taste

1 Place the peanuts and olive oil in a medium saucepan and cook over medium-low heat, stirring occasionally, until the peanuts start to brown, 10 to 15 minutes.

2 Add the remaining ingredients and cook, stirring occasionally, until the garlic and shallot have browned and all of the excess moisture has evaporated. Remove the pan from heat and let the mixture cool slightly.

3 Strain the mixture, reserving the oil. Using a mortar and pestle, grind the solids coarsely. Stir in the oil, season the salsa with salt, and use as desired.

Yield: 2 to 4 Servings
Active Time: 30 Minutes
Total Time: 24 Hours

Poule Nan Sos

4 bone-in, skin-on chicken thighs

1 tablespoon white vinegar

2 tablespoons fresh lemon juice

6 tablespoons Epis (see page 104)

2 teaspoons adobo seasoning

½ teaspoon black pepper

2 teaspoons garlic powder

Juice of ½ lime

2 tablespoons canola oil

1½ tablespoons tomato paste

1 red bell pepper, stem and seeds removed, sliced

1 green bell pepper, stem and seeds removed, sliced

1 small onion, sliced

6 sprigs of fresh parsley

6 sprigs of fresh thyme

8 whole cloves

1 habanero chile pepper

1 chicken bouillon cube, crushed

Salt, to taste

White rice, for serving

One of my favorite dishes from Haitian cuisine, and one of my favorite comfort foods. So many flavors are developed through the process of making poule nan sos that what is at heart a simple stewed chicken becomes unimaginably bold and complex.

1 Remove the skin from the chicken and score the meat with a paring knife, cutting to the bone to allow the marinade to work itself into the meat. Place the chicken in a bowl, add the vinegar and lemon juice, and rub them into the chicken. Drain the chicken, place it back in the bowl, and add ¼ cup of the Epis. Toss until the chicken is completely coated, cover the bowl with plastic wrap, and let the chicken marinate in the refrigerator overnight.

2 Place the chicken in a Dutch oven and season it with the adobo, black pepper, garlic powder, and lime juice, and stir until well combined. Cover the pot and place it over medium heat. Cook the chicken, turning it every 4 minutes, until it is cooked through, 15 to 20 minutes.

3 Remove the chicken from the pot and place it on a paper towel–lined plate to drain. Pour the pan juices into a bowl and set them aside.

4 Place the Dutch oven over medium-high heat and wait until any residual liquid has evaporated. Add the canola oil and warm it. Pat the chicken dry and carefully place it in the pot. Sear the chicken until browned all over.

5 Add the tomato paste and remaining Epis to the pot and cook, stirring continually, for 1 to 2 minutes.

6 Add half of the bell peppers and the onion to the pot and cook for 1 minute. Stir the reserved pan juices into the pot.

7 Tie the parsley and thyme together with kitchen twine. Poke the cloves into the habanero. Add the herbs, habanero, and bouillon cube to the pot and stir until well combined.

8 Taste the broth and adjust the seasoning as necessary.

9 Reduce the heat to medium-low and cook for 4 to 5 minutes. Taste and adjust the seasoning as necessary.

10 Stir in the remaining peppers and cook, stirring occasionally, until the chicken is very tender, 20 to 25 minutes. Take care not to pierce the habanero when stirring.

11 Taste and season the stew with salt. Ladle the stew over rice and serve.

Summer

Summer is synonymous with abundance. Fresh produce is plentiful, available seemingly everywhere. There are endless opportunities to get together with friends and family. Impromptu trips to the shore, to the lake, and to the mountains become commonplace, as we no longer wait for the weekend to start living.

In the rush to take advantage of this bounty, however, we tend to stretch ourselves too thin, preventing ourselves from truly appreciating how easy it is to be happy once the summer arrives. These dishes intend to temper that urge to go, go, go, reminding you that the best days of summer are those where you sit back with no plan and let things take whatever shape they please.

Full of flavor thanks to the spices, and subtly but surprisingly rich thanks to the ricotta and buttermilk, you won't hear anyone complaining if you decide to show up to the family barbeque with this cornbread. Cast iron adds rustic appeal, but this same recipe will do just fine in a 13 x 9–inch baking dish if that's your preference.

Skillet Cornbread

½ cup unsalted butter

3 eggs

2 tablespoons brown sugar

1 cup cornmeal

1 cup all-purpose flour

1 tablespoon baking powder

1½ teaspoons fine sea salt

½ teaspoon mustard powder

1 teaspoon chili powder

½ cup honey

1 cup buttermilk

2 tablespoons whole-milk ricotta cheese

1 Place the butter in a large skillet and melt it over medium heat. Cook the butter until it starts to brown and give off a nutty aroma. Remove the pan from heat and let the brown butter cool completely.

2 Preheat the oven to 325°F and position a rack in the center. Coat a large cast-iron skillet with nonstick cooking spray.

3 Place the eggs and brown sugar in the work bowl of a stand mixer fitted with the whisk attachment and whisk on high until the mixture is pale and fluffy.

4 Place the cornmeal, flour, baking powder, salt, mustard powder, and chili powder in a mixing bowl, stir to combine, and set the mixture aside.

5 Add the brown butter, honey, buttermilk, and ricotta to the stand mixer's work bowl and whisk until incorporated. Add the dry mixture and whisk until the mixture comes together as a smooth batter.

6 Pour the batter into the skillet and place it in the oven. Bake until a cake tester inserted into the center of the cornbread comes out clean, about 35 minutes.

7 Remove the cornbread from the oven and invert it onto a wire rack. Let the cornbread cool slightly before slicing and serving.

Though I am a big fan of cooking steak over an open fire, I am just as partial to the crust that is achieved by searing steak in a cast-iron pan. Chimichurri was made for steak, and using arugula's famed peppery bite in place of the fresh herb that traditionally serves as the foundation makes this dish a refreshing spin on the classic steak au poivre.

NY Strip
with Arugula Chimichurri

1 lb. NY strip steaks

Salt and pepper, to taste

2 tablespoons extra-virgin olive oil

2 tablespoons unsalted butter

2 sprigs of fresh thyme

2 garlic cloves, smashed

1 shallot, halved

Arugula Chimichurri (see page 85)

Baby arugula, for garnish

1 Preheat the oven to 475°F. Place the steaks on a paper towel–lined plate, season them with salt, and let them sit at room temperature. Pat the steaks occasionally with paper towels to remove the moisture that pools on top.

2 Warm a large cast-iron skillet over high heat. Place the olive oil in the pan, season the steaks with pepper, and place them in the pan.

3 Sear the steaks for 1 minute on each side. Add the butter, thyme, garlic, and shallot and use a large spoon to baste the steaks with the butter for 1 minute.

4 Transfer the steaks to the oven and roast until they are medium-rare (their interiors are 125°F), about 3 minutes. Remove the steaks from the oven and let them rest for 5 minutes.

5 Slice the steaks and season them with salt. Drizzle the chimichurri over the steaks, garnish with arugula, and serve.

Yield: 1 Cup
Active Time: 5 Minutes
Total Time: 5 Minutes

Chimichurri will most often be served alongside red meat, but in truth it is wonderful on just about everything. Parsley, basil, and other soft herbs usually provide the base, but I've found that the spicy character of arugula makes for a bold version.

Arugula Chimichurri

½ cup chopped arugula

1½ teaspoons chopped fresh oregano

1 small shallot, diced

1 small clove garlic, minced

2 tablespoons red wine vinegar

Salt and pepper, to taste

½ cup extra-virgin olive oil

1 Place all of the ingredients, except for the olive oil, in a mixing bowl and whisk to combine.

2 While whisking continually, slowly stream in the olive oil until it has emulsified.

3 Taste the chimichurri, adjust the seasoning as necessary, and either use immediately or store it in the refrigerator.

Yield: 6 Servings
Active Time: 5 Minutes
Total Time: 15 Minutes

In Haitian culture we refer to this version of a sweet treat as tablet nwa (nwa is the Creole word for cashew). A popular item that is commonly sold in markets or by street vendors in Haiti, I also offer it at my Haitian restaurant.

Cashew Pralines

1½ cups brown sugar

1 tablespoon cinnamon

1½ teaspoons ground ginger

1 teaspoon freshly grated nutmeg

½ cup water

2½ tablespoons unsalted butter

1½ tablespoons fresh lime juice

2 cups raw cashews

Coarse sea salt, for topping

1 Line a baking sheet with parchment paper. Place all of the ingredients, except for the cashews and salt, in a medium saucepan and bring to a boil.

2 Add the cashews and reduce the heat to medium. Stir until the caramel thickens almost to the point that you can't stir anymore.

3 Remove the pan from heat and check the temperature. It should be about 265°F. Spread the mixture onto the baking sheet and sprinkle salt over the top. Let the mixture cool completely before cutting it into individual servings.

Yield: 1 Serving
Active Time: 5 Minutes
Total Time: 5 Minutes

The combination of coconut, lime, and pineapple is so powerful that it allows the Piña Colada to weather every shift in what's fashionable. While it's hard to improve upon, that trio provides one a lot of room to play around in, and I've found that charring the pineapple makes the drink even more summery.

Charred Pineapple Piña Colada

2 pineapple wedges

5 fresh mint leaves, plus more for garnish

2 oz. lightly aged rum

1½ oz. coconut milk

1½ oz. pineapple juice

1 oz. Simple Syrup (see page 39)

½ oz. fresh lime juice

1 Using a kitchen torch, lightly char the pineapple wedges.

2 Place one of the charred pineapple wedges and the mint in a cocktail shaker and muddle.

3 Add the remaining ingredients, fill the cocktail shaker halfway with ice, and shake vigorously for 10 seconds.

4 Fill a highball glass with crushed ice and strain the cocktail over it.

5 Garnish with the remaining charred pineapple wedge and additional mint and enjoy.

Yield: 4 Servings
Active Time: 15 Minutes
Total Time: 45 Minutes

This dish is inspired by my love for elotes, or Mexican street corn, a simple preparation that checks every box—sweetness from the corn, richness and creaminess from the cotija and crema, and plenty of spice. Every time I cook with corn, I love to begin by steaming it within its own husk, which retains the moisture and amplifies the flavor while also honoring the ingredient.

Grilled Corn
with Cilantro Crema & Cotija Cheese

4 ears of corn

Unsalted butter, melted, as needed

2 tablespoons chopped fresh cilantro, plus more for garnish

1 cup sour cream

½ teaspoon kosher salt

1 teaspoon sugar

2 teaspoons fresh lime juice

1 teaspoon lime zest

½ teaspoon smoked paprika

¼ teaspoon cayenne pepper

1 cup crumbled cotija cheese

1 Prepare a gas or charcoal grill for medium-high heat (about 450°F).

2 Remove only the outermost layer of the corn's husks and place the corn on the grill. Cook, turning occasionally, until it is tender and charred all over.

3 Remove the corn from the grill, remove the husks, and place it back on the grill. Brush the corn with butter and cook until it has charred slightly. Remove the corn from the grill and set it aside.

4 Place all of the remaining ingredients, except for the cotija, in a food processor and blitz until combined.

5 Drizzle the crema over the corn, top it with the cotija, garnish with additional cilantro, and serve.

Yield: 2 to 4 Servings
Active Time: 20 Minutes
Total Time: 35 Minutes

In southern New Hampshire, we're blessed to have a number of incredible farms in the area, and this bit of fortune becomes impossible to ignore when the peaches begin to arrive, as the air becomes saturated with their sweet and floral scent. I soon start thinking about ways to incorporate that fruit as much as I can, and this salad is one of many realizations.

Grilled Peach Salad
with Lemon & Honey Vinaigrette

For the Salad

4 peaches, halved and pitted

2 tablespoons extra-virgin olive oil

Salt and pepper, to taste

6 oz. ciliegine mozzarella cheese

½ cup pistachios, toasted

1 cup cherry tomatoes, halved

Fresh basil leaves, for garnish

For the Vinaigrette

Juice and zest of 2 lemons

2 teaspoons honey

½ teaspoon Dijon mustard

2 teaspoons minced shallot

4 large fresh basil leaves, torn

½ teaspoon kosher salt

¼ teaspoon black pepper

⅓ cup extra-virgin olive oil

1 Prepare a gas or charcoal grill for medium-high heat (about 450°F).

2 To begin preparations for the salad, brush the cut sides of the peaches with the olive oil, season them with salt and pepper, and place them on the grill, cut side down. Cook until the peaches are lightly charred and have softened, 1 to 2 minutes.

3 Remove the peaches from the grill and let them cool.

4 To prepare the vinaigrette, place all of the ingredients, except for the olive oil, in a small bowl and whisk to combine. While whisking continually, slowly stream in the olive oil until it has emulsified.

5 Place the mozzarella, pistachios, and tomatoes in a bowl, add some of the vinaigrette, and toss to combine.

6 Arrange the peaches and mozzarella mixture on a serving platter, drizzle the remaining vinaigrette over the salad, garnish with basil, and serve.

Part of throwing a backyard barbeque is putting on a show, and if you really want to impress your friends and family, you'll make your own burger buns. The buttermilk makes for a fluffier bun, and the seeds add texture and a bit of umami.

Seeded Buttermilk Buns

½ cup buttermilk

2 cups all-purpose flour, plus more as needed

¾ teaspoon fine sea salt

¾ teaspoon active dry yeast

2½ tablespoons sugar

2 eggs

4 tablespoons unsalted butter, softened, plus more as needed

1 teaspoon milk

¼ cup mixed seeds (white and black sesame seeds, flaxseeds, poppy seeds)

1 Place the buttermilk in the work bowl of a stand mixer fitted with the dough hook. Add the flour, salt, yeast, sugar, 1 egg, and the butter and mix on low until combined.

2 Raise the speed to high and mix until the mixture comes together as a smooth, elastic dough.

3 Coat a large bowl with butter, form the dough into a ball, and place it in the bowl. Cover the bowl with plastic wrap and let the dough rise in a naturally warm spot until it has doubled in size, about 30 minutes.

4 Line a baking sheet with parchment paper. Place the dough on a flour-dusted work surface and cut it into 3½-oz. pieces. Roll them into tight balls and place them on the baking sheet, leaving at least 2½ inches of space between them. Cover the buns with a kitchen towel and place them in a naturally warm spot until they have doubled in size, about 30 minutes.

5 Preheat the oven to 325°F.

6 Place the remaining egg and the milk in a bowl and whisk to combine. Brush the buns with the egg wash and sprinkle the seeds over the top.

7 Place the buns in the oven and bake until they are golden brown, 20 to 25 minutes.

8 Remove the buns from the oven and let them cool before serving.

Yield: 4 Servings
Active Time: 20 Minutes
Total Time: 40 Minutes

A burger is wonderful in its classic form, but it is also very accommodating, allowing the imaginative cook to incorporate their favorite flavors and ingredients. These burgers are a perfect example, freighted with the flavors that make Haitian food so special.

If you're looking for an added kick, top these with Pikliz (see page 63) or Sos Ti Malice (see page 203).

Creole Smash Burgers

1 lb. ground beef

1 tablespoon Epis (see page 104)

2 tablespoons diced bell pepper

2 tablespoons diced onion

1 teaspoon adobo seasoning

2 teaspoons garlic powder

1 teaspoon black pepper, plus more to taste

Salt, to taste

3 tablespoons canola oil

4 slices of cheddar cheese

2 tablespoons unsalted butter

4 Seeded Buttermilk Buns (see page 94), split open

Spiced Mayonnaise (see opposite page)

8 slices of bacon, cooked

1 Place the ground beef, Epis, bell pepper, onion, adobo seasoning, garlic powder, and black pepper in a mixing bowl, season with salt, and stir until well combined.

2 Divide the mixture into 4½ oz. portions, form them into balls, and set them aside.

3 Place the canola oil in a large skillet and warm it over medium-high heat. Season the tops of the burgers with salt and pepper and place them in the pan, seasoned side down. If your pan is not large enough to comfortably fit all of the burgers at once, cook them in batches, as you want to provide them plenty of room in the pan.

4 Using a small skillet or a burger press, smash the burgers flat. Season the tops of the burgers with salt and pepper as they cook. Sear the burgers until they are browned, 2 to 3 minutes.

5 Flip the burgers over and sear on the other side, 2 to 3 minutes.

6 Top each burger with a slice of cheese. Cook until the burgers are cooked through and the cheese has melted, 3 to 5 minutes.

7 Remove the burgers from the pan, place them on a plate, and tent with aluminum foil to keep them warm.

8 Spread the butter on the cut sides of the buns. Place them in a large skillet and toast until just browned, 1 to 2 minutes.

9 Spread the Spiced Mayonnaise over the buns, assemble the burgers with the patties and bacon, and serve.

Yield: 1¼ Cups
Active Time: 5 Minutes
Total Time: 5 Minutes

Featuring Epis, Pikliz brine, and adobo seasoning, this mayo has plenty of heat, but the creamy and tangy qualities that are fundamental to the base of this spread make sure that potent element finds the mark.

Spiced Mayonnaise

1 tablespoon Epis
(see page 104)

1 cup mayonnaise

2 tablespoons ketchup

2 teaspoons Pikliz brine
(see page 63)

1 tablespoon sliced scallion

1 teaspoon adobo seasoning

1 teaspoon garlic powder

½ teaspoon sazon

½ teaspoon paprika

¼ teaspoon cayenne pepper

1 Place all of the ingredients in a bowl and stir until well combined.

2 Use immediately or store the mayonnaise in the refrigerator.

Creole Smash Burgers, see page 96

Yield: 1 Cake
Active Time: 20 Minutes
Total Time: 1 Hour and 30 Minutes

As my workdays typically start early and end late, it's not uncommon that you'll find me depending on an afternoon coffee to keep going. A cup of coffee cries out for a pastry, and coffee cake is one of my go-tos—I even enjoy those incredibly sweet ones you'd find at a gas station. Those don't compare to the taste and crumb of this homemade version, however.

Coffee Cake

For the Filling

¾ cup brown sugar

¾ cup all-purpose flour

2 teaspoons cinnamon

For the Streusel Topping

6 tablespoons unsalted butter, melted

1 cup brown sugar

1½ tablespoons cinnamon

1 cup all-purpose flour

For the Cake

1 cup unsalted butter

1 cup sugar

⅔ cup brown sugar

1 teaspoon fine sea salt

1 tablespoon baking powder

3⅔ cups all-purpose flour

1 tablespoon pure vanilla extract

¾ cup sour cream

1¼ cups milk

3 eggs

1 Preheat the oven to 350°F. To prepare the filling, place all of the ingredients in a bowl, stir to combine, and set it aside.

2 To prepare the streusel topping, place all of the ingredients in a bowl, stir to combine, and set it aside.

3 To begin preparations for the cake, place the butter and sugars in the work bowl of a stand mixer fitted with the paddle attachment and beat until the mixture is pale and fluffy, scraping down the work bowl with a rubber spatula as necessary.

4 Place the salt, baking powder, and flour in a separate bowl, whisk to combine, and set the mixture aside.

5 Add the vanilla, sour cream, and milk to the stand mixer's work bowl and beat until incorporated. Incorporate the eggs one at a time, beating until each one has been incorporated.

6 With the mixer running, gradually add the flour mixture and beat until it comes together as a smooth batter.

7 Coat a 13 x 9–inch baking pan with nonstick cooking spray and pour half of the batter into it. Sprinkle the filling over it and top with the remaining batter.

8 Sprinkle the streusel topping over the cake and place it in the oven. Bake until a cake tester inserted into the center of the cake comes out clean, about 35 minutes.

9 Remove the cake from the oven and let it cool slightly before slicing and serving.

As a chef, it's not unusual for people to ask about my earliest memories in the kitchen, and I always answer that I vividly recall sitting on the floor as a toddler, grinding up herbs and spices with my mom's mortar and pestle for epis. A close look through the book will show the weight that moment carries, as epis appears numerous times. A Haitian spice blend commonly used to marinate meat or seafood, it is a preparation I turn to again and again in my cooking.

Epis

8 scallions, trimmed

½ bunch of fresh parsley

1½ oz. garlic cloves, chopped

¼ large onion, chopped

1 tablespoon fresh thyme

¼ red bell pepper

¼ green bell pepper

¼ yellow bell pepper

¼ orange bell pepper

¼ habanero chile pepper

2 tablespoons extra-virgin olive oil

Juice of ½ lime

Salt, to taste

1 Place all of the ingredients in a blender and pulse until the mixture is a coarse paste.

2 Taste, adjust the seasoning as necessary, and pulse until smooth.

3 Use the epis immediately or store it in the refrigerator.

Yield: 1 Drink
Active Time: 5 Minutes
Total Time: 5 Minutes

On its face, this is just a spicy spin on the Margarita. But the addition of Pikliz brine adds a vegetal note that makes for a unique cocktail experience.

Feeling Hot Hot Hot

1 lime wedge, for the rim

Sea salt, for the rim

Chili powder, for the rim

1½ oz. tequila

½ oz. Ancho Reyes chile liqueur

¾ oz. fresh lime juice

2 oz. mango puree

½ oz. Pikliz brine (see page 63)

1 Rub the rim of a cocktail glass with the lime wedge. Combine the salt and chili powder in a small dish and coat the rim of the cocktail glass with the mixture. Chill the cocktail glass in the freezer.

2 Place the remaining ingredients in a cocktail shaker, fill it halfway with ice, and shake vigorously for 10 seconds.

3 Strain the cocktail into the chilled glass and enjoy.

Yield: 1 Cup
Active Time: 5 Minutes
Total Time: 5 Minutes

When I first started on my journey to becoming a chef, I did a stage (the industry term for internship) at a Boston restaurant. I was asked to create a dish for the chefs to taste and I made something that incorporated an herb-based oil. One of the chefs said that they could teach me how to make my oil far more vibrant. This is that vibrant oil, which retains the lively feeling I had at that moment.

Herb Oil

½ cup fresh basil
½ cup fresh parsley
½ cup chopped fresh chives
⅓ cup extra-virgin olive oil

1 Place a small metal bowl over a larger metal bowl that is filled with ice water.

2 Place all of the ingredients in a blender and puree on high until you see the olive oil start smoke, about 1 minute.

3 Warm a small skillet over high heat. When the pan is hot, remove it from heat and carefully pour the oil into the pan. Place the pan back over high heat and cook the oil for about 20 seconds, until the bubbles in the oil start to become smaller.

4 Immediately transfer the oil to the small bowl sitting in the ice bath. Stir the oil until it is cold to the touch.

5 Strain the oil through a coffee filter or cheesecloth, letting it slowly drip through. Discard the solids and use the oil immediately.

Yield: 2 to 4 Servings
Active Time: 30 Minutes
Total Time: 3 Hours

At one of the farms we work closely with, there is a team of Jamaicans who grow some of the best produce around. On weekends they sell jerk chicken at the farm, and an early encounter with it sparked my imagination, resulting in this tribute, which is a marriage of Jamaican and Haitian flavors.

Jerk Chicken Wings

For the Chicken Wings

2 lbs. chicken wings

¼ cup plus 1 tablespoon Jerk Spice Blend (see page 112)

2 cups all-purpose flour

Salt, to taste

Canola oil, as needed

For the Sauce

1 cup ketchup

1 tablespoon Jerk Spice Blend

1 teaspoon fresh lime juice

2 teaspoons Sos Ti Malice (see page 203)

2 teaspoons brown sugar

1 To begin preparations for the chicken wings, place the chicken in a bowl, add ¼ cup of Jerk Spice Blend, and toss to combine. Place the chicken in the refrigerator and let it marinate for 2 hours.

2 Place the flour and remaining Jerk Spice Blend in a shallow bowl and stir to combine. Set the mixture aside.

3 Add canola oil to a Dutch oven until it is about 2 inches deep and warm it to 325°F.

4 Remove the chicken wings from the refrigerator and dredge them in the seasoned flour until they are completely coated.

5 Working in batches to avoid crowding the pot, gently slip the chicken wings into the hot oil. Fry until they are crispy and their interior temperature is 165°F.

6 Transfer the fried chicken wings to a paper towel-lined plate and season them with salt.

7 To prepare the sauce, place all of the ingredients in a bowl and whisk until well combined.

8 Drizzle the sauce over the chicken wings or serve it alongside as a dipping sauce.

You'll want to start using this with chicken, but once you taste the results of this blend, you'll be tempted to "jerk" everything.

Jerk Spice Blend

1 tablespoon onion powder

1 tablespoon garlic powder

1 tablespoon dried thyme

1 tablespoon adobo seasoning

2 teaspoons sazon

2 teaspoons cayenne pepper

2 teaspoons kosher salt

2 teaspoons black pepper

1 tablespoon allspice

1 tablespoon paprika

1 teaspoon red pepper flakes

1 teaspoon cumin

2 teaspoons cinnamon

½ teaspoon nutmeg

1 teaspoon ground cloves

1 teaspoon ground ginger

1 cup Epis (see page 104)

1 tablespoon browning sauce

1 Place all of the ingredients in a mixing bowl, stir to combine, and use immediately or store in an airtight container.

With a lean cut like pork tenderloin, I prefer to use a spice rub that will enhance the flavor and also create a beautiful crust on the exterior. The lack of fat also makes pork loin easy to overcook, so it's best to cook until the interior is 130°F and let the meat come to the desired temperature as it rests, as that will ensure a moist, tender, and enjoyable result.

Grilled Pork Loin
with Green Goddess Pesto

2 (½ lb.) portions of center-cut pork tenderloin

2 teaspoons kosher salt, plus more to taste

1 teaspoon black pepper

1 teaspoon smoked paprika

1 teaspoon onion powder

½ teaspoon garlic powder

½ teaspoon cumin

½ cup Green Goddess Pesto (see page 30)

1 Prepare a gas or charcoal grill for medium heat (about 400°F).

2 Pat the pork dry with paper towels. Place the remaining ingredients, except for the pesto, in a bowl, stir to combine, and season the pork with the mixture.

3 Place the pork on the grill and cook until the interior temperature is about 130°F, turning it as necessary.

4 Remove the pork from the grill and let it rest for 10 minutes, which should bring the interior up to 140°F.

5 Slice the pork, season it with salt, drizzle the pesto over the top, and serve.

Few desserts are as suitable to summer as a lemon meringue pie. With the cooling look of the meringue and refreshing taste of the lemon custard, a slice is a fitting capper to a great summer day.

Lemon Meringue Pie

Quick Pastry Dough
(see page 54)

All-purpose flour, as needed

For the Filling

1½ cups fresh lemon juice

1 tablespoon lemon zest

4 egg yolks

1 cup sugar

¼ cup cornstarch

4 tablespoons unsalted butter, cubed

For the Meringue

½ cup water

1 cup sugar

4 egg whites

¼ teaspoon cream of tartar

1 Place the dough on a flour-dusted work surface and roll it out into a 13-inch round that is about ¼ inch thick. Coat a 9-inch pie plate with nonstick cooking spray, place the dough in it, and chill the dough in the refrigerator for 30 minutes.

2 Preheat the oven to 350°F. Remove the crust from the refrigerator, trim away any excess dough, and crimp the edge. Place a piece of parchment paper in the crust and fill it with baking weights or dried beans. Place the crust in the oven and blind bake it for about 10 to 15 minutes.

3 Remove the crust from the oven, remove the chosen weight and parchment, and return the crust to the oven. Bake until the crust is golden brown, 10 to 15 minutes. Remove the crust from the oven and let it cool completely.

4 To begin preparations for the filling, place the lemon juice and lemon zest in a small saucepan and bring to a simmer.

5 Place the egg yolks, sugar, and cornstarch in a bowl and whisk until well combined. When the lemon mixture has come to a simmer, add half of it to the egg mixture, whisking continually. Add the tempered mixture to the saucepan and cook over medium heat until the custard has thickened. Be careful not to overcook the custard or it will become grainy.

6 Remove the pan from heat and whisk in the butter. Pour the filling into the cooled piecrust and place a piece of plastic wrap directly on the surface of the custard to prevent a skin from forming. Place the pie in the refrigerator.

7 To begin preparations for the meringue, place the water and sugar in a small saucepan and bring to a boil, stirring to dissolve the sugar. Continue cooking until the syrup is 240°F.

8 While waiting for the syrup to warm up, place the egg whites and cream of tartar in the work bowl of a stand mixer fitted with the whisk attachment and whip on high until the mixture holds stiff peaks.

9 With the mixer running, slowly stream in the syrup. Whip until the meringue has cooled and holds stiff peaks.

10 Remove the pie from the refrigerator and remove the plastic. Spread the meringue over the filling and use the spatula to create peaks. Using a kitchen torch, carefully toast the meringue until golden brown. Serve immediately.

Yield: 1 Cup

Active Time: 5 Minutes

Total Time: 5 Minutes

As a chef, a number of the dishes that I prepare for family gatherings start at the restaurant. This sweetened butter took the opposite route, becoming a fixture at one of our restaurants after it received favorable reviews at a small party.

Molasses & Honey Butter

1 cup unsalted butter, softened

2 teaspoons molasses

2 tablespoons honey

Coarse sea salt, to taste

1 Place the butter, molasses, and honey in a bowl and stir until well combined.

2 Transfer the butter to a serving dish, sprinkle coarse sea salt over the top, and serve.

This simple preparation is destined to become one that you are never without, as its sweet and tart crunch is at home on a number of dishes.

Pickled Red Onion

1 large red onion, sliced

2 cups red wine vinegar

1 teaspoon fennel seeds

1 teaspoon mustard seeds

½ teaspoon celery seeds

⅓ cup sugar

1 teaspoon kosher salt

1 Place the onion in a mason jar. Place the remaining ingredients in a small saucepan and bring to a boil, stirring to dissolve the sugar and salt.

2 Pour the brine over the onion, making sure it is completely submerged, and let it cool completely before serving or storing in the refrigerator.

A jar of these will be a great inclusion on a cheese board, but they are also wonderful on a salad or alongside grilled meats.

Pickled Carrots

2 cups apple cider vinegar

¼ cup sugar

2 teaspoons coriander seeds

1 teaspoon fennel seeds

½ teaspoon red pepper flakes

½ teaspoon fine sea salt

2 large carrots, peeled and sliced thin

1 Place all of the ingredients, except for the carrots, in a small saucepan and bring to a boil.

2 Place the carrots in a mason jar and pour the brine over them.

3 Set the pickled carrots aside and let them cool completely before serving or storing in the refrigerator.

Yield: 2 to 4 Servings
Active Time: 45 Minutes
Total Time: 24 Hours

Rinsing rice to remove some of the starch before cooking it is the key to getting the fluffy result you want every time.

Diri Kole

½ cup dried kidney beans, soaked overnight

2 tablespoons canola oil

1 tablespoon Epis (see page 104)

2 teaspoons adobo seasoning

2 teaspoons garlic powder

2 teaspoon kosher salt

1 cup basmati rice, rinsed well

1 Drain the beans and place them in a small saucepan. Cover them with about 4 cups of water and bring to a boil. Reduce the heat so that the beans simmer and cook until they are tender, 45 to 50 minutes.

2 Drain the beans, reserving the cooking liquid.

3 Place the canola oil in a large skillet and warm it over medium heat. Add the Epis and cook, stirring, for 1 minute.

4 Add the kidney beans, adobo, garlic powder, and salt and stir to combine.

5 Add 1½ cups of the reserved cooking liquid to the pan and bring to a boil.

6 Add the rice and gently stir to incorporate. Reduce the heat to low and cover the pan. Cook until the rice is tender and has absorbed all of the cooking liquid.

7 Remove the pan from heat and let the rice and beans sit, covered, for 5 minutes before serving.

Tacos are too important to restrict to one day of the week. For me, they are one of the most versatile dishes out there, filled with endless possibilities. The tostada is an open-faced taco that was created as a way to use up stale tortillas, and its crunch is welcome in this bright and fresh iteration.

Yield: 4 Servings
Active Time: 30 Minutes
Total Time: 2 Hours and 30 Minutes

Octopus Tostadas

For the Octopus

8 cups water

3 oranges, halved

3 limes, halved

½ bunch of fresh parsley

2 shallots, chopped

5 garlic cloves, smashed

2 tablespoons coriander seeds

1 tablespoon black peppercorns

5 lb. octopus

For the Scallion Mayo

½ cup mayonnaise

1 teaspoon fresh lime juice

1 tablespoon sliced scallion greens

1 tablespoon chopped fresh parsley

Canola oil, as needed

12 corn or flour tortillas

Salt and pepper, to taste

Paprika, to taste

1 cup Red Chermoula Sauce (see page 66)

Fresh cilantro, topped, for garnish

Pickled Carrots (see page 124), for garnish

1 cup crumbled cotija cheese, for garnish

1 To prepare the octopus, place all of the ingredients, except for the octopus, in a large pot and bring to a boil. Carefully lower the octopus in the pot and reduce to a simmer. Cook until the tentacles are tender, about 1½ hours.

2 Prepare an ice bath and place the octopus in it.

3 To prepare the scallion mayo, place all of the ingredients in a bowl, stir to combine, and set it aside.

4 Add canola oil to a Dutch oven until it is about 1 inch deep and warm it to 350°F. Add the tortillas to the hot oil 1 at a time and fry until they are crispy, 1 to 2 minutes. Remove the tostadas from the oven, transfer them to a paper towel–lined plate to drain and season them with salt and paprika. Keep the oil at 350°F.

5 Remove the octopus from the ice bath, remove the tentacles, and pat them completely dry with paper towels. Add the tentacles one at a time to the hot oil and fry until they are crispy, 2 to 3 minutes. Transfer the fried tentacles to a paper towel–lined plate, let them drain, and season with salt and pepper.

6 When the tentacles are cool enough to handle, cut them into bite-size pieces.

7 Spread the mayo over the tostadas and top it with octopus. Drizzle the chermoula over the top and garnish with cilantro, the Pickled Carrots, and cotija.

I can never get enough of the rich and creamy flavor of peanut butter, and employing it in an ice cream amplifies its sweet side. For ice cream lovers who do not have an ice cream maker—it's time to invest. Once you do, get in the habit of storing the mixing bowl in the freezer for 24 hours before you are going to make ice cream in it.

Peanut Butter Ice Cream

1 cup creamy peanut butter

¾ cup sugar

1 cup whole milk

2 cups heavy cream

2 teaspoons pure vanilla extract

¼ teaspoon fine sea salt

1 Place all of the ingredients in a mixing bowl and stir until well combined.

2 Pour the mixture into an ice cream maker and churn until it has the desired consistency, about 35 minutes.

3 Transfer the ice cream to an airtight container, cover it, and let it set in the freezer for about 5 hours before enjoying.

Shrimp cocktail has far more room for imagination than most people think, as it is an accessible preparation that can still be plated elegantly and paired with unique sauces.

Head-On Shrimp Cocktail

with Chive Puree & Lemon Mayonnaise

For the Shrimp

8 cups water

3 lemons, halved

1 tablespoon black peppercorns

1 tablespoon fennel seeds

1 tablespoon red pepper flakes

¼ bunch of fresh parsley

2 shallots, chopped

¼ cup garlic cloves, smashed

2 tablespoons kosher salt

15 head-on shrimp, shells removed, deveined

For the Puree

Salt, to taste

½ lb. fresh chives

1 lemon peel

1 shallot, sliced

1 garlic clove, sliced

¼ cup canola oil

Lemon Mayonnaise (see page 133), for serving

Cocktail Sauce (see page 132), for serving

1 Prepare an ice bath. To prepare the shrimp, place all of the ingredients, except for the shrimp, in a large pot and bring to a boil. Add the shrimp and poach until they are cooked through, 2 to 3 minutes.

2 Drain the shrimp, plunge them into the ice bath, and drain again. Place the shrimp on a paper towel–lined plate to dry.

3 Prepare another ice bath. To prepare the puree, bring water to a boil in a medium saucepan. Add salt, the chives, lemon peel, shallot, and garlic and cook for 1 to 2 minutes. Remove the mixture with a strainer, plunge it into the ice bath, and drain. Squeeze the mixture to remove excess moisture and place it in a blender. With the blender running, slowly stream in the canola oil until it has emulsified. Taste the puree and adjust the seasoning as necessary.

4 To serve, place the shrimp on a plate and dot the plate with the puree and Lemon Mayonnaise. Serve with the Cocktail Sauce and enjoy.

Yield: 1 Cup
Active Time: 5 Minutes
Total Time: 5 Minutes

Great with shrimp, or with oysters on the half-shell, this sauce will make a summer day spent at home feel like an occasion.

Cocktail Sauce

1 cup ketchup

1 tablespoon grated fresh horseradish

Juice and zest of 1 lemon

1 tablespoon sliced fresh chives

Pinch of salt

Pinch of black pepper

1 Place all of the ingredients in a bowl and stir to combine.

2 Use immediately or store the sauce in the refrigerator.

Yield: 1 Cup
Active Time: 5 Minutes
Total Time: 5 Minutes

The rich flavor of mayonnaise is just asking to be spiked with a bright element such as lemon zest.

Lemon Mayonnaise

1 cup mayonnaise

Zest of 2 lemons

1 Place all of the ingredients in a bowl and stir to combine.

2 Use immediately or store the mayonnaise in the refrigerator.

I am a big fan of contrasting textures being present in an ingredient, and these smashed potatoes accomplish this difficult task, combining the creamy interior of a boiled potato with the crispy exterior of French fries. As the fresh herbs and summer beans lighten the dish, I'm frying the potatoes, but for a healthier preparation, toss the potatoes in olive oil after smashing them and roast them in the oven at a high temperature to achieve an exterior that won't be too far off from what you'd get deep-frying the potatoes.

Smashed Potatoes

with Summer Beans, Pancetta, Parmesan & Herbs

1½ lbs. baby potatoes

Salt, to taste

5 garlic cloves, smashed

3 sprigs of fresh thyme

1 tablespoon black peppercorns

½ lb. summer beans, trimmed and cut into thirds

4 oz. pancetta, diced

Canola oil, as needed

½ cup grated Parmesan cheese

1 Rinse the potatoes under cold water and place them in a large pot. Cover them with water and add about 2 tablespoons of salt, the garlic, thyme, and peppercorns. Bring to a boil and then reduce the heat so that the water simmers. Cook until the potatoes are fork tender, 15 to 20 minutes.

2 Drain the potatoes and place them on paper towels to dry.

3 While the potatoes are cooking, bring water to a boil in a medium saucepan and prepare an ice bath. Add salt until the water tastes like sea water (about 3 tablespoons) and the beans and cook for 1 minute.

4 Drain the beans and plunge them into the ice bath. Drain the beans again, place them in a mixing bowl, and set them aside.

5 Place the pancetta in a small skillet and cook over medium-low heat, stirring occasionally, until the fat has rendered and the pancetta is crispy, about 6 minutes. Remove the pan from heat and set it aside.

6 Gently smash the potatoes to flatten them and pat them completely dry with paper towels.

7 Add the pancetta to the mixing bowl containing the beans.

8 Add canola oil to a large, deep cast-iron skillet until it is about ½ inch deep and warm it to 325°F. Working in batches to avoid crowding the pot, gently slip the smashed potatoes into the hot oil and fry on each side until the potatoes are golden brown, turning them as necessary.

9 Remove the lightly fried potatoes from the oil and add them to the mixing bowl. Season with salt and pepper, toss to combine, and transfer them to a serving dish.

10 Top the dish with the Parmesan and serve immediately.

Yield: 2 Servings
Active Time: 20 Minutes
Total Time: 30 Minutes

Plums are a wonderful fruit to work with, as they are great raw, roasted, or caramelized, and always look enticing on the plate.

Caramelized Plums
with Fennel, Orange, Ginger Yogurt & Pine Nuts

1 cup champagne vinegar or white wine vinegar

½ cup fresh orange juice

3 tablespoons sugar, plus more as needed

½ teaspoon fine sea salt, plus more to taste

½ bulb of fennel, trimmed and shaved thin

2 tablespoons minced fresh ginger

½ cup Greek yogurt

2 tablespoons unsalted butter

3 ripe plums, halved and pitted

Fennel Pesto (see page 140)

1 cara cara orange, peeled and sliced, for garnish

1 Place the vinegar, orange juice, sugar, and salt in a small saucepan and bring to a boil. Place the shaved fennel in a mason jar and pour the hot brine over it. Cover the jar with plastic wrap and let the fennel pickle.

2 Place the ginger and yogurt in a bowl and stir to combine.

3 Place the butter in a large skillet and melt it over medium heat. Place sugar in a shallow bowl and coat the cut sides of the plums with it. Place the plums in the pan, cut side down, and cook until they are caramelized.

4 Chop the plums and season them with salt. Place them in a bowl, add the pickled fennel, and toss to combine.

5 Spread the yogurt over the bottom of a serving dish.

6 Arrange the plums and pickled fennel on top, drizzle the Fennel Pesto over the salad, garnish with the orange, and serve.

Yield: 2½ Cups
Active Time: 15 Minutes
Total Time: 15 Minutes

In the summer, fennel becomes a workhorse, as it is able to bolster simple salads and tame other bold flavors. Consider using some fennel fronds in this pesto to amplify the freshness and anise flavor.

Fennel Pesto

¾ cup pine nuts

1 cup chopped fennel greens

½ cup fresh parsley

10 fresh mint leaves

1 teaspoon fine sea salt

½ teaspoon black pepper

1 teaspoon fresh lemon juice

Zest of 1 lemon

¼ cup canola oil

1 tablespoon extra-virgin olive oil

1 Preheat the oven to 350°F. Place the pine nuts on a baking sheet and place them in the oven. Toast the pine nuts until they are fragrant and browned, about 6 minutes. Remove the pine nuts from the oven and set them aside.

2 Place the toasted pine nuts and all of the remaining ingredients, except for the oils, in a food processor and blitz to combine. With the food processor running, slowly stream in the oils until they have emulsified.

3 Taste the pesto, adjust the seasoning as necessary, and use immediately or store it in the refrigerator.

Yield: 2 Servings
Active Time: 10 Minutes
Total Time: 10 Minutes

This sandwich takes inspiration from one of my favorites, the Cuban, which is typically made with garlic and citrus-marinated pork, Swiss, ham, and pickles. Here, the pork will be spicier and tangier, differences that take this sandwich in a wonderful direction.

V.O. Griot

V.O. Griot Spread
(see page 146)

2 Adobo Brioche Buns
(see page 157), split open

½ lb. Griot (see page 184)

4 slices of ham

4 slices of Swiss cheese

½ cup Pikliz (see page 63)

1 Preheat a panini press.

2 Spread the griot spread over the buns, divide the Griot, ham, cheese, and Pikliz between them, and assemble the sandwiches.

3 Toast the sandwiches in the panini press until they are golden brown and the cheese has melted. Serve immediately.

Yield: 1 Cup
Active Time: 5 Minutes
Total Time: 5 Minutes

Sour orange juice comes from Seville oranges, and its uniquely vibrant flavor makes it a tremendous ingredient in sauces, dressings, marinades, and spreads.

V.O. Griot Spread

2 teaspoons sour orange juice

1 cup mayonnaise

1 teaspoon fresh lime juice

1 tablespoon chopped parsley

1 Place all of the ingredients in a mixing bowl and stir to combine.

2 Use the spread immediately or store it in the refrigerator.

Yield: 6 Servings
Active Time: 15 Minutes
Total Time: 2 Hours

If you are planning to break up this meringue to top a dessert like the Red Velvet Cake on page 150, leave the peppercorns a little more coarse when grinding them. If you want to serve the meringues by themselves, grind them finely.

Pink Peppercorn Meringue

½ cup water

1 cup sugar

4 egg whites

¼ teaspoon cream of tartar

1 tablespoon pink peppercorns, ground

1 tablespoon cacao nibs, ground

Cocoa powder, for topping

1 Preheat the oven to 250°F and line a baking sheet with parchment paper. Place the water and sugar in a small saucepan and bring to a boil, stirring to dissolve the sugar. Cook until the syrup reaches 240°F.

2 While the syrup is warming, place the egg whites and cream of tartar in the work bowl of a stand mixer fitted with the whisk attachment and whip on high until the mixture holds stiff peaks.

3 With the mixer running, slowly stream the syrup into the work bowl. Whip on high until the meringue has cooled and holds stiff peaks.

4 Spread the mixture in a thin layer on the baking sheet. Sprinkle the pink peppercorns, cacao nibs, and cocoa powder over the meringue and place it in the oven.

5 Bake until the meringue is set, 20 to 30 minutes. Turn the oven off and allow the meringue to dry in the oven for 45 minutes.

6 Remove the meringue from the oven and use immediately or store in an airtight container.

Red velvet cake gets its red hue from the interaction between the cocoa powder, buttermilk, and vinegar, a characteristic that is then enhanced by the addition of red food coloring. A number of stories have become attached to this cake, but the one I relate to most is its connection to Juneteenth, where the color red is used as a representation of those enslaved people who were killed before they ever had an opportunity to experience freedom.

Red Velvet Cake

For the Cake

2½ cups all-purpose flour

1 teaspoon baking soda

1 teaspoon fine sea salt

4 teaspoons cocoa powder

2 eggs

1½ cups sugar

1½ cups canola oil

⅓ cup whole milk

1 cup crème fraîche

1 to 2 tablespoons red gel food coloring

1 teaspoon white vinegar

2 teaspoons pure vanilla extract

Unsalted butter, as needed

For the Mousse

1½ teaspoons powdered gelatin

6 egg yolks

1 cup sugar

1 lb. mascarpone cheese

1 lb. cream cheese, softened

2 teaspoons pure vanilla extract

Pink Peppercorn Meringue (see page 149), for topping

1 Preheat the oven to 350°F. To begin preparations for the cake, sift the flour, baking soda, salt, and cocoa powder into a mixing bowl and stir to combine. Set the mixture aside.

2 Place the eggs and sugar in the work bowl of a stand mixer fitted with the paddle attachment and beat until pale and fluffy.

3 Add the canola oil, milk, crème fraîche, food coloring, vinegar, and vanilla to the work bowl and beat until combined.

4 Gradually add the dry mixture to the wet mixture and beat until it comes together as a smooth batter.

5 Coat two 10-inch cake pans with butter and divide the batter between the pans. Tap them on a counter to evenly distribute the batter and remove any air bubbles.

6 Place the cakes in the oven and bake until a cake tester inserted into their centers comes out clean, 25 to 35 minutes. Remove the cakes from the oven and let them cool completely in their pans.

7 To begin preparations for the mousse, place the gelatin and 1 tablespoon water in a glass and let the gelatin bloom.

8 Fill a medium saucepan halfway with water and bring it to a simmer. Place the egg yolks and sugar in a heatproof bowl, place it over the simmering water, and whisk continually. Whisk in the gelatin mixture and remove the pan from heat.

9 Place the mascarpone, cream cheese, and vanilla in a mixing bowl and stir until combined. Add the mascarpone mixture to the egg yolk mixture, fold to incorporate, and cover the bowl with plastic wrap. Place the mousse in the refrigerator and chill until it has cooled completely.

10 Remove the cakes from the pans and cut them in half at their equators. Spread some of the mousse on top of one piece, place another piece on top, and top with more of the mousse. Repeat with another piece of cake and the mousse. Place the last piece of cake on top and either spread the remaining mousse over the top, or place it in a piping bag fitted with a star tip and decorate the top of the cake with it. Break up the meringue, sprinkle it over the top, and enjoy.

Fall

Spring and summer are hopeful, joyous seasons, bursting with life. But they are also uniform, predictable, marching in a single direction. There are many reasons to love autumn, but one of the biggest is that each day contains the potential for a surprise, and within the course of a single week one can drive out to the shore for a lobster roll and an ice cream cone, spend an evening nursing a Margarita while tending the grill, and also spend a cozy day wrapped in a sweater, alternating between tending to a soup simmering on the stove and a good book, grateful to be sheltered from the cold rain outside. Fall is a perfect blend of all the seasons, an irresistible mix framed in glory.

Radicchio has a tendency to be overlooked—most people's familiarity with it is limited to its inclusion in a salad mix. A crisp chicory, its bitter flavor lends itself to being grilled or roasted in the oven.

Grilled Radicchio
with Tahini & Dill Caesar Dressing

2 heads of radicchio, quartered

1 tablespoon extra-virgin olive oil

1 tablespoon fresh lemon juice

2 tablespoons chopped fresh parsley

1 tablespoon chopped fresh dill

Tahini & Dill Caesar Dressing (see page 156)

Parmesan cheese, shaved, for garnish

Lemon zest, for garnish

Toasted sesame seeds, for garnish

Croutons, for garnish

1 Prepare a gas or charcoal grill for medium-high heat (about 450°F). Place the radicchio, olive oil, lemon juice, parsley, and dill in a mixing bowl and toss to combine.

2 Place the radicchio on the grill and cook, turning it as necessary, until it is tender and lightly charred. Remove the radicchio from the grill and set it aside.

3 Place the radicchio in a serving dish and drizzle the dressing over it. Garnish with Parmesan, lemon zest, toasted sesame seeds, and croutons and serve.

A creamy, refreshing dressing that is great at taming boldly flavored vegetable dishes.

Tahini & Dill Caesar Dressing

2 tablespoons tahini paste

¼ cup grated Parmesan cheese

1 teaspoon black pepper

1½ teaspoons kosher salt

3 anchovies in olive oil, drained

Zest of 1 lemon

2 tablespoons fresh lemon juice

3 egg yolks

1 tablespoon Dijon mustard

¾ cup canola oil

1 tablespoon chopped fresh dill

1 Place all of the ingredients, except for the canola oil and dill, in a food processor and blitz to combine.

2 With the food processor running, slowly stream in the canola oil until it has emulsified.

3 Taste the dressing and adjust the seasoning as necessary. Add the dill and pulse until it has been incorporated. Use immediately or store the dressing in the refrigerator.

To me, the irresistible egg and butter–enriched brioche resides somewhere between a pastry and a bread, and this allows it to work equally well in sweet or savory preparations. You can also keep the dough together, bake it in a loaf pan, and use it for sandwiches or serve it alongside your favorite soup.

Adobo Brioche Buns

½ cup lukewarm water (90°F)

¾ teaspoon active dry yeast

2 cups all-purpose flour, plus more as needed

¾ teaspoon fine sea salt

½ teaspoon garlic powder

1 teaspoon adobo seasoning

2½ tablespoons sugar

2 eggs

4 tablespoons unsalted butter, softened

Extra-virgin olive oil, as needed

1 teaspoon milk

1 Place the water in the work bowl of a stand mixer fitted with the dough hook. Add the yeast, gently stir, and let the mixture sit until it starts to foam, about 10 minutes.

2 Add the flour, salt, garlic powder, adobo, sugar, 1 egg, and the butter and mix on low until the flour has been incorporated. Raise the speed to high and mix until the mixture comes together as a smooth, elastic dough, 3 to 4 minutes.

3 Coat a large bowl with olive oil, place the dough in the bowl, and cover it with plastic wrap. Let the dough rise in a naturally warm spot until it has doubled in size, about 30 minutes.

4 Line a baking sheet with parchment paper. Place the dough on a flour-dusted work surface and cut it into 6 or 8 evenly sized pieces, depending on the size of the buns you prefer.

5 Roll the pieces into tight balls and place them on a baking sheet. Cover the buns with a kitchen towel and let them rise in a naturally warm spot until they have doubled in size, about 1 hour.

6 Preheat the oven to 325°F.

7 Place the milk and remaining egg in a bowl and whisk to combine. Brush the buns with the egg wash and place them in the oven.

8 Bake the buns until they are golden brown, 20 to 25 minutes. Remove the buns from the oven, transfer them to a wire rack, and let them cool before serving.

Yield: 3 Cups
Active Time: 25 Minutes
Total Time: 2 Hours

Imagine the flavor of applesauce: light, fresh, and crisp with subtle spice. Now think of a bolder, more concentrated version, and you have apple butter. The name refers to this spread's texture rather than the presence of butter, as it is smooth and creamy. Be sure to keep the skin on the apples for full flavor, and if you prefer a more savory spread, reduce the amount of sugar.

Apple Butter

3 cups brandy

5 lbs. apples, rinsed well

½ cup real maple syrup

¼ cup brown sugar

1 teaspoon fine sea salt

½ teaspoon cinnamon

¼ teaspoon coriander

¼ teaspoon ground cloves

¼ teaspoon nutmeg

1 Place the brandy in a saucepan, bring it to a boil over medium-high heat, and cook until it has reduced by half, about 15 minutes. Remove the pan from heat and set it aside.

2 Cut the apples into quarters, remove the cores, place them in a stockpot, and cover them with cold water. Bring to a boil over medium-high heat and then reduce the heat so that the apples simmer. Cook until tender, about 15 minutes, and then drain.

3 Preheat the oven to 225°F. Run the apples through a food mill and catch the pulp in a mixing bowl. Add the reduced brandy and the remaining ingredients, stir to combine, and transfer the mixture to a shallow baking dish.

4 Place the baking dish in the oven and bake the apple mixture, stirring every 10 minutes or so, until all of the excess water has evaporated, 1 to 1½ hours.

5 Remove the baking dish from the oven, transfer the mixture to a food processor, and blitz until smooth. Use immediately or store in the refrigerator.

Yield: 4 to 6 Servings
Active Time: 30 Minutes
Total Time: 1 Hour and 30 Minutes

Poke is a popular Hawaiian dish that is served as an appetizer or entree and is typically made with tuna. I wanted to take the unique flavors of the dish and use them in a vegetarian preparation, and beets ended up being a perfect fit, as they have a color and texture similar to tuna. If you need to bring a dish to a get-together, this recipe is a great one to turn to, as it can be prepared a day in advance and it travels well.

Beet Poke
with White Soy Vinaigrette

For the Beet Poke

3 red beets

3 golden beets

3 pink baby beets

6 sprigs of fresh thyme

6 garlic cloves

3 tablespoons extra-virgin olive oil

3 tablespoons soy sauce

6 tablespoons water

For the Vinaigrette

2 tablespoons rice vinegar

2 teaspoons honey

1 teaspoon Dijon mustard

2 teaspoon white soy sauce

½ teaspoon black pepper

1 teaspoon sesame oil

¾ cup canola oil

White rice, cooked and cooled to room temperature, for serving

Radishes, sliced thin, for garnish

Sesame seeds, toasted, for garnish

Scallion greens, sliced thin, for garnish

1 Preheat the oven to 400°F. To begin preparations for the beet poke, group the beets according to color and place each group in a separate aluminum foil pouch. Divide the remaining ingredients between the pouches, seal them, and place them in a baking pan.

2 Place the pouches in the oven and roast the beets until a knife inserted into them passes easily to their centers, 45 minutes to 1 hour.

3 Remove the beets from the oven and let them cool.

4 When the beets are cool enough to handle, peel them and cut them into bite-size pieces. Place the beets in a bowl and let them cool completely.

5 To prepare the vinaigrette, place all of the ingredients, except for the canola oil, in a small bowl and whisk to combine. While whisking continually, slowly stream in the canola oil until it has emulsified. Taste the vinaigrette and adjust the seasoning as necessary.

6 Add the vinaigrette to the beet poke and toss to combine. Serve over white rice and garnish with sliced radishes, toasted sesame seeds, and sliced scallion greens.

Yield: 1½ Cups
Active Time: 5 Minutes
Total Time: 25 Minutes

When I'm on the hunt for a sweet-and-salty snack, candied nuts is my go-to. This is a good recipe to get in the habit of making when you're going to be spending some time in the kitchen doing meal prep, as they are great for snacking, as good on top of salads as they are on ice cream, and amazing as part of a charcuterie board.

Candied Pecans

1½ cups pecans

¼ cup water

¾ cup sugar

½ teaspoon fine sea salt

¾ teaspoon cinnamon

¼ teaspoon ground ginger

1 Preheat the oven to 350°F and line a baking sheet with parchment paper. Place the pecans on another baking sheet and place them in the oven. Toast the pecans until they are fragrant, about 6 minutes. Remove the pecans from the oven and set them aside.

2 Place the remaining ingredients in a medium saucepan and bring to a boil, stirring to dissolve the sugar. Cook the syrup until it is 235°F.

3 Add the toasted pecans and stir until they are coated. Place the pecans on the parchment-lined baking sheet and let them cool completely before serving.

Yield: 1 Serving
Active Time: 5 Minutes
Total Time: 5 Minutes

Any red wine that you're partial to will work here, but I've found that Zinfandels and Malbecs are the best options. Floating the rum-fortified wine on top of the cocktail is purely for aesthetics—you could just as easily maintain these ratios, combine everything in a large pitcher, and serve this sangria to a big crowd.

Tropical Sangria

5 oz. red wine

½ oz. lightly aged rum

½ apple, chopped

2 orange slices, plus more for garnish

1 oz. pineapple juice

1 oz. orange juice

½ oz. apple juice

Apple slices, for garnish

1 Place the wine and rum in a mixing glass and stir to combine.

2 Place ice, the apples, oranges, and juices in a wineglass and stir until combined.

3 Float the wine mixture on top by slowly pouring it over the back of a spoon.

4 Garnish with apple slices and additional orange slices and enjoy.

Yield: 4 to 6 Servings
Active Time: 10 Minutes
Total Time: 10 Minutes

A gathering doesn't need to start off with a cheese board, but to me it seems that the best ones do. A board is accessible, versatile, and brings people together in a way that encourages conversation. With so many interesting cheeses out there, it is tougher than ever to decide what's going to go on a board, and I typically try and include a soft cheese, a boldly flavored blue cheese, and a hard cheese. Also, remember that while there are not many rules when composing a board, it is essential that the cheese be at room temperature when you serve it.

Cheese Board

4 to 6 oz. blue cheese

4 to 6 oz. Manchego cheese

4 to 6 oz. camembert cheese

12 slices of bread, toasted

¼ cup Apple Butter
(see page 158)

½ cup Candied Pecans
(see page 162)

½ cup Pickled Carrots
(see page 124)

½ cup honeycomb

¼ cup whole-grain mustard

1 Arrange the ingredients on a serving board in an aesthetically appealing manner and serve.

Yield: 4 Servings
Active Time: 30 Minutes
Total Time: 45 Minutes

The key to making potato chips at home is running the thinly sliced potatoes under cold water, which removes some of the starch and prevents them from browning before they have a chance to become crispy in the hot oil. This is my preferred seasoning blend, but go with whatever flavors you find appealing—even a standard combination of salt and pepper are great on a crispy chip.

Homemade Potato Chips

Canola oil, as needed

2 medium Idaho potatoes

2 medium sweet potatoes

2 teaspoons paprika

1 teaspoon vinegar powder

2 tablespoons fine sea salt

1 tablespoon black pepper

1 Add canola oil to a Dutch oven until it is about 2 inches deep and warm it to 300°F.

2 Using a mandoline, cut the potatoes into thin rounds and place them in a container. Cut the sweet potatoes into thin rounds and place them in a separate container.

3 Rinse the potatoes and sweet potatoes under cold water for 30 seconds.

4 Place the paprika, vinegar powder, salt, and pepper in a small bowl, stir to combine, and set the mixture aside.

5 Drain the potatoes and sweet potatoes and pat them dry with paper towels.

6 Working in batches to avoid crowding the pot, gently slip the potatoes into the pot and fry until they are crispy and golden brown. Repeat with the sweet potatoes.

7 As the potato and sweet potato chips finish cooking, use a slotted spoon to transfer them to a mixing bowl lined with paper towels. Season them with the spice mixture, toss to combine, and transfer them to a serving bowl. Serve once all of the chips have been cooked and seasoned.

Yield: 1 Loaf
Active Time: 30 Minutes
Total Time: 21 Hours

My bread-making journey began with rustic loaves like this one. I read many books, experimented with my own recipes, and eventually my passion for the art of baking resulted in me opening a bakery. As precision is paramount in the bread-making process, I have also given the measurements here by weight.

Artisanal Country Bread

12.3 oz. (350 g) all-purpose flour, plus more as needed

5.3 oz. (150 g) whole wheat flour

13.2 oz. (375 g) lukewarm water (90°F)

¼ (scant) teaspoon (500 mg) active dry yeast

⅓ oz. (11 g) fine sea salt

1 Place the flours and water in a large mixing bowl and work the mixture until it comes together as a dough. Cover the bowl with a kitchen towel and let the mixture rest for 45 minutes to 1 hour.

2 Sprinkle the yeast and salt over the dough and fold to incorporate them. Cover the bowl with the kitchen towel and let it rest for 30 minutes.

3 Remove the kitchen towel, fold a corner of the dough into the center, and cover the bowl with the kitchen towel. Repeat every 30 minutes until all of the corners have been folded in to the center of the dough. After the last fold, cover the bowl with the kitchen towel and let the dough rest at room temperature for 12 to 14 hours.

4 Place the dough on a flour-dusted work surface and fold each corner of the dough to the center. Turn the dough over and roll it into a smooth ball. Be careful not to press on the dough too hard, as this will deflate it and prevent it from expanding properly in the oven.

5 Dust a bowl with flour and place the dough, seam side down, in the bowl. Cover the bowl with a kitchen towel and let the dough rise until it has doubled in size, about 1 hour and 15 minutes.

6 Cut a circle that is 1 inch larger than the circumference of a Dutch oven out of a piece of parchment paper. When the dough has approximately 1 hour remaining in its rise, preheat the oven to 475°F, cover the Dutch oven, and place it in the oven as it warms.

7 Invert the dough onto a flour-dusted work surface and score the top with a razor or very sharp knife. Carefully remove the Dutch oven from the oven. Use a bench scraper to transfer the dough onto the piece of parchment. Carefully lower the dough into the Dutch oven. Cover the Dutch oven, place it in the oven, and bake the bread for 20 minutes.

8 Remove the Dutch oven's lid and bake the loaf until it is golden brown and sounds hollow when tapped, about 20 minutes.

9 Remove the bread from the oven and let it cool on a wire rack for at least 2 hours before slicing.

When breaking cod down into fillets to serve at my restaurants, I often find myself with a lot of meat that can't be served as is, but, obviously, can't be thrown away. One of the best ways to deploy these odds and ends is in a chowder, which will warm the hearts of all who encounter it.

Cod Chowder

Salt and white pepper, to taste

1 potato, peeled and chopped

½ lb. bacon, chopped

½ cup unsalted butter

1 large onion, diced

1 cup diced celery

2 carrots, peeled and diced

¾ cup all-purpose flour

2 cups seafood stock or vegetable stock

1 cup heavy cream

2 cups whole milk

1 lb. cod, chopped

1 teaspoon paprika

½ teaspoon cayenne pepper

1 tablespoon fresh lemon juice

1 Bring water to a boil in a large saucepan. Add salt and the potato and parboil until it is almost tender, about 10 minutes. Drain the potato and set it aside.

2 Place the bacon in a Dutch oven and cook it over medium heat, stirring occasionally, until the fat has rendered and it is crispy, about 8 minutes.

3 Add the butter, onion, celery, and carrots, season with salt and white pepper, and cook, stirring occasionally, until the onion is translucent, about 3 minutes.

4 Add the flour and stir continually until the flour begins to brown and gives off a nutty aroma.

5 Add the stock, cream, and milk and bring to a gentle simmer. Cook until the flour develops to your liking and the broth thickens, 15 to 20 minutes.

6 Add the cod, reduce the heat to low, and cook until it is cooked through, 8 to 10 minutes.

7 Stir in the potato, paprika, cayenne, and lemon juice and cook until the potato is tender, about 5 minutes.

8 Taste, adjust the seasoning as necessary, and serve.

Yield: 12 to 16 Bars
Active Time: 20 Minutes
Total Time: 1 Hour and 30 Minutes

Cheesecake is beloved by many, but many of those folks would never thinking of attempting to make it at home, as it is notoriously finicky. These bars are a great entry point into the cheesecake-baking process, and are also wonderful for a get-together away from your house, as they are easier to transport.

Cheesecake Bars
with Chocolate Ganache

For the Crust

1⅓ cups graham cracker crumbs

⅓ cup brown butter (see page 43)

¼ cup sugar

For the Filling

4 cups cream cheese, softened

1 cup sugar

1 cup sour cream

2 teaspoons pure vanilla extract

1½ teaspoons fresh lemon juice

3 eggs

For the Ganache

¾ cup chocolate chips

½ cup heavy cream

1 Preheat the oven to 350°F. To prepare the crust, place all of the ingredients in a mixing bowl and stir to combine. Press the mixture into the bottom and slightly up the sides of a 13 x 9–inch baking dish, using the bottom of a measuring cup to pack it down.

2 Place the crust in the oven and bake it until it is set, about 8 minutes. Remove the crust from the oven and set it aside. Leave the oven on.

3 To prepare the filling, place the cream cheese and sugar in the work bowl of a stand mixer fitted with the paddle attachment and beat for 2 minutes. Add the sour cream, vanilla, and lemon juice and beat to incorporate. Incorporate the eggs 1 at a time, scraping down the work bowl as needed.

4 Spread the filling over the baked crust and cover the baking dish with aluminum foil. Place the baking dish in a large roasting pan and add hot water until it reaches about 1 inch up the sides of the baking dish. Cover the roasting pan with aluminum foil and place it in the oven.

5 Bake the bars for 45 minutes. Turn off the oven, crack the oven door, and let the bars rest in the cooling oven for 1 hour.

6 To prepare the ganache, place the chocolate chips in a heatproof bowl. Place the cream in a small saucepan and bring it to a simmer. Pour the warm cream over the chocolate chips and stir until combined. Cover the bowl with plastic wrap and let the ganache cool in the refrigerator.

7 Remove the bars from the oven and chill them in the refrigerator for 2 hours before spreading the ganache over the top, slicing, and serving.

Yield: 4 to 6 Muffins
Active Time: 10 to 15 Minutes
Total Time: 2 Hours

I had no idea how easy making English muffins was until I opened a bakery and wanted my own version to use for the breakfast sandwiches we served. With just a little patience, you too can start turning out these fluffy, irresistible muffins and transform the next brunch you host.

English Muffins

¾ cup milk

1½ tablespoons unsalted butter, softened, plus more as needed

¾ teaspoon fine sea salt

2½ teaspoons sugar

1 egg

1⅔ cups all-purpose flour, plus more as needed

1 teaspoon active dry yeast

Semolina flour, as needed

1 Place the milk in a small saucepan and warm over medium heat until it just comes to a simmer. Place it in the work bowl of a stand mixer fitted with the dough hook and add all of the remaining ingredients, except for the semolina flour.

2 Work the mixture on low speed to combine. Raise the speed to medium and work the mixture until it is a smooth dough, about 3 minutes.

3 Coat a large bowl with butter, place the dough in it, and cover it with plastic wrap. Let the dough rise in a naturally warm spot until it has doubled in size, about 1 hour.

4 Warm a cast-iron skillet over low heat. Dust a work surface with all-purpose flour and place the dough on it. Roll it out into a ¾-inch-thick rectangle and cut it into 3-inch rounds.

5 Dust the tops and bottoms of each round with semolina and place them in the warm pan. Cook until the English muffins are golden brown on both sides, 6 to 8 minutes, turning them over halfway through.

6 Remove the English muffins from the pan and let them cool slightly before serving.

Yield: 2 to 4 Servings
Active Time: 10 Minutes
Total Time: 50 Minutes

One thing I love so much about delicata squash is that, unlike other fall and winter squashes, delicata does not need to be peeled, as the skin is—you guessed it—delicate. Poaching it in olive oil honors this delicate quality, grilling it briefly adds a slightly smoky element, and the Spiced Pepitas lend the dish a beautiful textural contrast.

Olive Oil– Poached Delicata Squash
with Apple Butter & Spiced Pepitas

4 cups extra-virgin olive oil

4 sprigs of fresh thyme

3 garlic cloves, crushed

1 sprig of fresh sage, plus more, chopped, for garnish

3 delicata squash, seeded and sliced into rings

Salt and pepper, to taste

Apple slices, for garnish

Spiced Pepitas (see opposite page), for garnish

1 cup Apple Butter (see page 158), for serving

1 Preheat the oven to 325°F. Place the olive oil, thyme, garlic, and sage in a small saucepan and warm the mixture over low heat.

2 Place the squash in a deep baking dish and pour the olive oil and herbs over it. Place the squash in the oven and roast until it is fork-tender, about 15 minutes.

3 Prepare a gas or charcoal grill for medium heat (about 400°F).

4 Remove the squash from the oven, remove them from the oil, and season them with salt and pepper. Reserve some of the oil.

5 Carefully place the squash on the grill and cook until it is charred on each side, turning them over once. Remove the squash from the grill, place it on a plate, and tent with aluminum foil to keep warm.

6 Place some of the reserved olive oil in a skillet and warm it over high heat. Add some chopped sage and fry it for 1 minute.

7 Transfer the squash to a serving dish, garnish with sliced apples, pepitas, and fried sage, and serve with the Apple Butter.

Yield: 1 Cup
Active Time: 5 Minutes
Total Time: 45 Minutes

When fall hits and pumpkins become readily available, this recipe becomes a fixture at home and in my restaurants. Great for topping salads, soups, and roasted vegetable dishes, these toasted pepitas supply an irresistible crunch. Advieh is a Persian spice blend that is similar in flavor to garam masala—if you can't track it down at the store, swap in that familiar Indian spice.

Spiced Pepitas

1 cup pepitas

1 tablespoon extra-virgin olive oil

2 teaspoons advieh

1 teaspoon salt

1 teaspoon black pepper

1 Preheat the oven to 325°F and line a baking sheet with parchment paper.

2 Place all of the ingredients in a bowl and toss to combine. Transfer the pepitas to the baking sheet, place them in the oven, and toast until they are golden brown, about 10 minutes.

3 Remove the pepitas from the oven and let them cool before using or storing in an airtight container.

Olive Oil–Poached Delicata Squash with Apple Butter & Spiced Pepitas, see page 180

Any real discussion of Haitian cuisine has to include griot, a fried pork dish that is a fixture at parties and festive family dinners. This recipe can work with a number of sides, but fried plantains and Pikliz (see page 63) are those that I turn to most often when I am serving griot.

Griot

2 lbs. pork shoulder, cubed

¼ cup Epis (see page 104)

2 tablespoons sour orange juice

2 tablespoons fresh lime juice

1½ tablespoons adobo seasoning

1½ tablespoons garlic powder

2 teaspoons sazon

Salt, to taste

6 sprigs of fresh parsley

6 sprigs of fresh thyme

8 whole cloves

1 habanero chile pepper

Canola oil, as needed

Bell peppers, chopped, for garnish

Red onion, chopped, for garnish

Shallot, chopped, for garnish

Fresh herbs, chopped, for garnish

Lime wedges, for serving

1 Place the pork, Epis, juices, adobo, garlic powder, and sazon in a bowl, season with salt, and toss to combine. Cover the bowl and let the pork marinate in the refrigerator for 6 to 7 hours.

2 Place the pork and marinade in a Dutch oven and add water until the pork is covered.

3 Tie the parsley and thyme with kitchen twine and add the bouquet garni to the pot. Poke the cloves into the habanero, add it to the pot, and bring to a boil.

4 Reduce the heat to medium and simmer the pork for 20 minutes.

5 Taste the liquid and adjust the seasoning as necessary. Cook until the pork is tender. Using a slotted spoon, transfer the pork to a paper towel–lined plate and let it drain.

6 Add canola oil to a large, deep skillet until it is about 1 inch deep and warm it to 350°F. Working in batches to avoid crowding the pan, add the pork and fry until it is crispy.

7 Transfer the fried griot to another paper towel–lined plate to drain.

8 Garnish the griot with peppers, onion, shallot, and fresh herbs and serve with lime wedges.

Yield: 4 Large Macaroons
Active Time: 15 Minutes
Total Time: 1 Hour

A preparation that will deceive your friends and family when they encounter it at a party—from the look and flavor, it seems like a dessert that requires considerable technique and a number of ingredients. In reality, it's incredibly simple and consists of items most people have in their pantry.

Coconut Macaroons

7 oz. sweetened shredded coconut

7 oz. sweetened condensed milk

½ teaspoon pure vanilla extract

1 large egg white, at room temperature

4 oz. dark chocolate chips

⅛ teaspoon fine sea salt, plus more for topping

1 Preheat oven to 325°F and line a baking sheet with parchment paper.

2 Place the coconut, milk, and vanilla in a small bowl and stir until well combined. Set the mixture aside.

3 Place the egg white in a bowl and whip it with a handheld mixer until it holds firm peaks.

4 Add the whipped egg white to the coconut mixture and fold to combine.

5 Using an ice cream scoop, scoop dollops of the batter onto the baking sheet.

6 Place the coconut macaroons in the oven and bake until they are golden brown, 25 to 30 minutes.

7 Remove the macaroons from the oven and let them cool completely.

8 Bring a few inches of water to a boil in a small saucepan. Place the chocolate chips in a heatproof bowl and place it over the simmering water. Stir the chocolate chips until they are melted and smooth.

9 Drizzle the melted chocolate over the macaroons, sprinkle salt over them, and enjoy.

This preparation is my take on the Alsatian sauerkraut known as choucroute. As it is not fermented, it does not have quite the same tang, but it possesses a fresh, crisp quality that makes it far more versatile.

Pickled Red Cabbage

½ cup red wine vinegar

¼ cup canola oil

⅔ cup sugar

1½ teaspoons kosher salt

1½ teaspoons dried mustard

1 teaspoon celery seeds

½ teaspoon mustard seeds

½ cup Roasted Chicken Stock (see page 214)

¼ head of red cabbage, shredded

1 Place all of the ingredients, except for the cabbage, in a medium saucepan and bring to a boil.

2 Add the cabbage and cook until it is tender, about 20 minutes.

3 Pour the cabbage and brine into a mason jar and let it cool completely before using or storing in the refrigerator.

If I had to choose just one bread to make sandwiches with, this would be the one. It is simple, but incorporating mashed potato transforms the crumb into a creamy, chewy wonder that makes even a sandwich composed of cold cuts memorable.

Potato Bread

¾ cup warm water (105°F)

2 teaspoons active dry yeast

3⅛ cups all-purpose flour, plus more as needed

1¼ teaspoons fine sea salt

3½ tablespoons sugar

6 tablespoons unsalted butter, softened

1 large egg

½ cup plain mashed potatoes, cooled to room temperature

1 Place all of the ingredients in the work bowl of a stand mixer fitted with the paddle attachment and mix on low until the mixture comes together as a dough. Raise the speed to high and work the dough until it is smooth and elastic, about 3 to 4 minutes.

2 Coat a large mixing bowl with nonstick cooking spray. Form the dough into a ball, place it in the bowl, and cover the bowl with plastic wrap. Let the dough rise in a naturally warm spot until it has doubled in size, about 1 hour.

3 Place the dough on a flour-dusted work surface and press it into a rough square. Fold the bottom third of the dough to the center then fold the top third to the center, overlapping the bottom third. Turn the dough and repeat the folds so that the dough will fit in a 9 x 5–inch loaf pan.

4 Coat a 9 x 5–inch loaf pan with nonstick cooking spray, place the dough in it, and let it rise until it has tripled in size, about 1 hour.

5 Preheat the oven to 350°F.

6 Place the bread in the oven and bake until it is golden brown and the internal temperature is 190°F to 200°F.

7 Remove the bread from the oven and gently invert the pan over a wire rack to remove the loaf. Let the bread cool completely before slicing and serving.

Though this is intended to be served warm on a crisp autumn day, it also works brilliantly as a chilled soup, meaning you can serve it as a second course in the summer. With a rich and creamy broth, and plenty of bright acidity thanks to the crème fraîche and sherry vinegar, this one is sure to have people feeling content when they push back from the table.

Potato & Leek Soup

½ cup unsalted butter

1 leek, white part only, rinsed well and sliced

1 small onion, sliced

5 garlic cloves, sliced

Salt, to taste

3 large potatoes, peeled and chopped

4 cups milk

1 teaspoon sherry vinegar

½ cup crème fraîche

½ cup heavy cream

1 Place the butter in a medium saucepan and melt it over medium heat. Add the leek, onion, and garlic, season with salt, and cook, stirring frequently, until the onion and leek are translucent, about 3 minutes.

2 Add the potatoes and milk, season with salt, and bring to a gentle simmer. Reduce the heat to low and cook until the potatoes are tender, 15 to 20 minutes.

3 Drain the vegetables, reserving the milk. Add the vegetables to a blender along with the sherry vinegar, crème fraîche, and cream and puree until smooth, adding the reserved milk as needed to get the desired consistency.

4 Taste the soup, adjust the seasoning as necessary, and serve.

When comfort is what you're after at a gathering, this elevated version of macaroni and cheese is the place to turn. The bell peppers and shallots add a subtle hint of sweetness, and the velvety, tangy sauce that results from the mayonnaise, evaporated milk, and cheeses supplies unparalleled flavor.

Rigatoni au Gratin

Salt, to taste

1 lb. rigatoni

½ cup unsalted butter

2 shallots, diced

½ cup diced bell pepper

3 cups evaporated milk

1½ cups grated Parmesan cheese

1½ cups grated gouda cheese

½ cup mayonnaise

2 teaspoons garlic powder

2 teaspoons adobo seasoning

1 Bring water to a boil in a large saucepan. Add salt and the pasta and cook until the pasta is al dente, 6 to 8 minutes. Drain the pasta and let it cool.

2 Preheat the oven to 375°F.

3 Place the butter in a large skillet and melt it over medium heat. Add the shallots and pepper and cook, stirring occasionally, until the shallots are translucent, about 3 minutes.

4 Add the evaporated milk, three-quarters of the cheeses, the mayonnaise, garlic powder, and adobo and stir continually until the cheeses have melted. Taste and adjust the seasoning as necessary.

5 Add the pasta and stir to combine.

6 Coat a baking dish with nonstick cooking spray. Pour the rigatoni mixture into the dish, making sure it is spread in an even layer.

7 Top with the remaining cheeses and place the dish in the oven. Bake until the top is golden brown, about 20 minutes.

8 Remove the gratin from the oven and let it cool slightly before serving.

Butterfly pea flowers are a wonderful ingredient to experiment with in your cocktail making, as they provide a vibrant, eye-catching purple hue, and also a sweet, floral character that is reminiscent of chamomile.

Purple Rèn

2 teaspoons butterfly pea flowers

4 oz. boiling water

1½ oz. gin

¼ oz. crème de violette

¼ oz. fresh lime juice

2 oz. orange juice

2 fresh basil leaves, torn, for garnish

1 Place the butterfly pea flowers and boiling water in a measuring cup and steep for 5 minutes. Strain the tea, pressing down on the flowers to extract as much liquid as possible. Place the tea in the refrigerator and let it cool completely.

2 Fill a rocks glass with ice.

3 Place 1 oz. of the butterfly pea tea and the remaining ingredients, except for the garnish, in a cocktail shaker, fill it halfway with ice, and shake vigorously for 15 seconds.

4 Strain over ice, garnish with the basil, and enjoy.

Yield: 2 Servings

Active Time: 30 Minutes

Total Time: 1 Hour

There are many blessings that come with running a restaurant, and building relationships with local mushroom foragers and growers is one. The fruits of their labors frequently guide what we do at the restaurant—and this hearty vegetarian main is one of the very best preparations to result from these connections. A surefire hit once the weather turns cooler.

Roasted King Trumpet Mushrooms

with Parsnips, Spinach & Brussels Sprouts

1 cup chopped parsnip

2 tablespoons extra-virgin olive oil

Salt and pepper, to taste

5 tablespoons canola oil

5 large king trumpet mushrooms, stems removed, halved and scored

4 teaspoons sherry vinegar

2 cups shiitake mushrooms, sliced

2 garlic cloves, minced

2 tablespoons minced shallot

1 tablespoon unsalted butter

2 cups spinach

1 cup Brussels sprout leaves

2 tablespoons chopped fresh parsley

1 Preheat the oven to 400°F. Place the parsnips in a mixing bowl, add the olive oil, season with salt and pepper, and toss to combine. Place the parsnips on a baking sheet and place them in the oven.

2 Roast the parsnips until they are tender, 10 to 15 minutes. Remove the parsnips from the oven and set them aside. Leave the oven on.

3 Place 3 tablespoons of the canola oil in a large cast-iron skillet and warm it over medium-high heat. Season the king trumpet mushrooms with salt and pepper and place them in the pan, cut side down. Cook until the edges begin to brown and then place the pan in the oven. Roast the mushrooms until they are tender, 5 to 8 minutes.

4 Remove the mushrooms from the oven and add half of the vinegar. Toss to coat the mushrooms and place them on a paper towel–lined plate to drain.

5 Place the remaining canola oil in a large skillet and warm it over medium-high heat. Add the shiitake mushrooms, season with salt and pepper, and cook until they are golden brown and crispy, about 8 minutes, stirring occasionally.

6 Add the garlic and shallot and cook, stirring continually, for 1 minute.

7 Add the butter and stir until the mushrooms are coated. Deglaze the pan with the remaining vinegar, scraping any browned bits up from the bottom.

8 Add the spinach, Brussels sprout leaves, and roasted parsnips and season with salt and pepper. Cook until the spinach and brussels sprout leaves have wilted.

9 Add the parsley and stir to combine.

10 Transfer the vegetables to a serving dish, top with the king trumpet mushrooms, and serve.

Yield: 2 Pints
Active Time: 10 Minutes
Total Time: 2 Days

These incredible pickles were inspired by a dish I encountered at a local restaurant and was quickly powerless to resist. Crisp, spicy, sweet, salty, and refreshing, they are positively addicting, and you'll soon be including them on charcuterie boards, serving them as a tapa with cocktails, or inserting them into your sandwiches.

Sichuan Pickled Cucumbers

4 cups rice vinegar

1 tablespoon kosher salt

½ cup sugar

1½ teaspoons mustard seeds

1 tablespoon coriander seeds

1 teaspoon black peppercorns

2 teaspoons Sichuan peppercorns

2 shallots, sliced

¼ cup garlic cloves, crushed

10 baby cucumbers, left whole or sliced on a bias

1 Place all of the ingredients, except for the cucumbers, in a medium saucepan and bring to a boil, stirring to dissolve the salt and sugar.

2 Place the cucumbers in mason jars. Pour the brine over them and let them cool completely.

3 Cover the jars and chill them in the refrigerator for 2 days before serving.

Yield: 2 Cups
Active Time: 10 Minutes
Total Time: 40 Minutes

As a proud person of Haitian descent, I may be biased, but for me, this is the king of hot sauces. It is spicy, of course, but sos ti malice is also sweet for a hot sauce, an element that makes it a go-to condiment for dishes served morning, noon, and night.

Sos Ti Malice

1 teaspoon extra-virgin olive oil

1 small onion, sliced

2 scotch bonnet chile peppers or 2 habanero chile peppers, stems and seeds removed, sliced

½ small red bell pepper, sliced

3 garlic cloves, sliced

Salt and pepper, to taste

2 tablespoons tomato paste

2 tablespoons apple cider vinegar

1 tablespoon fresh lime juice

1 cup water, plus more as needed

1 Place the olive oil in a medium saucepan and warm it over medium heat. Add the onion, chiles, bell pepper, and garlic, season with salt and pepper, and cook for about 5 minutes.

2 Add the remaining ingredients and bring to a boil. Reduce the heat so that the mixture simmers and cook for about 20 minutes.

3 Transfer the mixture to a blender and puree on high until it is smooth. Add water as desired to achieve the right consistency.

4 Taste the hot sauce, adjust the seasoning as necessary, and use immediately or store it in the refrigerator.

Yield: 4 to 6 Servings
Active Time: 20 Minutes
Total Time: 45 Minutes

Squash Bisque

Keep an eye out for unique squashes at your local farmers market or upscale grocery store, as this simple bisque will be a wonderful landing spot for them. While I recommend using Spiced Pepitas to add more levels of flavor, you can also just salvage the seeds from the squash, toast them in the oven, and use them as a garnish. If it's important that you keep the dish vegetarian, use vegetable stock in place of the Roasted Chicken Stock.

3 tablespoons unsalted butter

1 large onion, sliced

5 garlic cloves, sliced

2 lbs. butternut squash, peeled, seeded, and chopped

Salt and pepper, to taste

5 cups Roasted Chicken Stock (see page 214)

1 cup milk

1 cup heavy cream

Spiced Pepitas (see page 181), for garnish

1 Place the butter in a medium saucepan and melt it over medium heat. Add the onion and garlic and cook, stirring continually, until they have softened, about 5 minutes.

2 Add the squash, season with salt and pepper, and then add the stock, milk, and cream.

3 Bring to a boil, reduce the heat, and let the mixture simmer until the squash is tender.

4 Strain the mixture, reserving the liquid.

5 Transfer the squash to a blender and puree on high until smooth, adding the reserved liquid as needed to reach the desired consistency.

6 Taste the bisque, adjust the seasoning as necessary, and ladle it into warm bowls. Garnish with the Spiced Pepitas and serve.

If you have friends and family who are vegan, this is a great entree to break out at a gathering, as it fits their restricted diet and is still sure to satisfy the omnivores at the table.

Roasted Cauliflower
with Green Romesco & Hazelnut Gremolata

2 tablespoons canola oil

1 large head of cauliflower, cut into ½-inch steaks

Salt and pepper, to taste

Green Romesco Sauce (see page 208)

Hazelnut Gremolata (see page 209)

1 Place the canola oil in a large skillet and warm it over medium-high heat. Working in batches to avoid crowding the pan, add the cauliflower and season it with salt and pepper. Cook until the cauliflower is golden brown on each side, 6 to 8 minutes, turning it over just once.

2 When all of the cauliflower has been cooked, place it in a serving dish, drizzle the Green Romesco Sauce over it, and sprinkle the Hazelnut Gremolata on top. Serve immediately.

In its classic Catalonian form, romesco would feature red bell peppers, but I've found that utilizing green bell peppers tamps down the sweetness just enough that the other elements present can shine.

Green Romesco Sauce

2 heads of garlic

¼ cup plus 2 teaspoons extra-virgin olive oil

2 large green bell peppers

½ bunch of fresh parsley

4 scallions, trimmed and chopped

½ cup toasted hazelnuts

2 teaspoons kosher salt

1 Preheat the oven to 400°F. Place each head of garlic in a square of aluminum foil, drizzle 1 teaspoon of olive oil over each one, and fold up the foil into a pouch.

2 Place the garlic and peppers on a baking sheet and place them in the oven. Roast until the peppers are charred all over, turning them as necessary, and the garlic cloves are tender and golden brown.

3 Remove the peppers from the oven, place them in a bowl, and cover it with a kitchen towel. Let them steam for 10 minutes. Remove the garlic from the oven and let it cool.

4 When the garlic is cool enough to handle, remove the cloves and place them in a blender. Remove the skin, stems, and seeds from the peppers and add the flesh to the blender. Add the parsley, scallions, hazelnuts, and salt and puree until smooth.

5 With the blender running, slowly stream in the remaining olive oil until it has emulsified. Taste the sauce, adjust the seasoning as necessary, and use immediately or store in the refrigerator.

Yield: ¾ Cup
Active Time: 10 Minutes
Total Time: 30 Minutes

This nutty blend adds wonderful texture to any dish, and also a surprising brightness, thanks to the lemon zest and shallots.

Hazelnut Gremolata

½ cup hazelnuts

1½ tablespoons extra-virgin olive oil

1 tablespoon chopped fresh parsley

2 teaspoons sliced fresh chives

1 tablespoon diced shallots

1 tablespoon lemon zest

1 tablespoon fresh lemon juice

1 Preheat the oven to 350°F. Place the hazelnuts on a baking sheet, place them in the oven, and toast until they are golden brown, about 6 minutes. Remove the hazelnuts from the oven and let them cool.

2 Chop the hazelnuts and place them in a bowl. Add the remaining ingredients and stir to combine.

3 Taste the gremolata, adjust the seasoning as necessary, and use as desired.

Spice blends are a great way to get people acquainted with the flavors of other cultures, and suya is a nutty mixture that is a key element of Nigerian cuisine. While it is traditionally used to marinade meats, I've found that it is an incredible weapon when you're looking to add depth to vegetable-centered dishes.

Suya-Spiced Carrots

60 rainbow carrots
(20 of each color), peeled and
rinsed well

3 tablespoons extra-virgin
olive oil

1½ tablespoons suya

2 teaspoons fine sea salt

3 garlic cloves, smashed

5 sprigs of fresh thyme

1 tablespoon fresh lemon juice

Handful of arugula

3 tablespoons crumbled
feta cheese

2 tablespoons toasted pine nuts

Pickled Red Onion
(see page 120), to taste

1 Preheat the oven to 425°F. Place the carrots on a large piece of aluminum foil and drizzle 1 tablespoon of the olive oil over them. Season with the suya and salt and toss to combine. Add the garlic and thyme and fold the aluminum foil over the carrots, creating a pouch.

2 Place the carrots in the oven and roast until they are tender, 25 to 45 minutes. Cook times can vary significantly depending on the thickness of the carrots.

3 Remove the carrots from the oven, transfer them to a serving dish, and set them aside.

4 Place the remaining olive oil and the lemon juice in a bowl and whisk to combine.

5 Place the vinaigrette and arugula in a bowl and toss to combine.

6 Add the dressed arugula to the serving dish along with the feta, pine nuts, and pickled onion. Toss to combine and serve immediately.

Yield: 16 Cups
Active Time: 1 Hour
Total Time: 24 Hours

Chicken stock is one of those items that should be in your refrigerator or freezer at all times, as it makes all the difference when making soups and sauces, or cooking grains. Get in the habit of saving chicken bones in your freezer, and when you have enough, roast them briefly in the oven to concentrate their flavor, and proceed with replenishing your supply of stock.

Roasted Chicken Stock

3 lbs. chicken bones

24 cups cold water

2 large onions, quartered

2 celery stalks, cut into large pieces

3 large carrots, peeled and cut into large pieces

1 tablespoon black peppercorns

2 teaspoons coriander seeds

1 bay leaf

2 sprigs of fresh thyme

4 sprigs of fresh parsley

3 garlic cloves, smashed

1 Preheat the oven to 400°F. Place the chicken bones on a baking sheet lined with aluminum foil. Place it in the oven and roast the chicken bones until they are browned, 10 to 15 minutes.

2 Remove the bones from the oven and place them in a stockpot. Cover them with the water and bring to a boil.

3 Reduce the heat so that the water simmers and skim the fat and impurities from the surface.

4 Add the remaining ingredients and simmer the stock until the flavor has developed to your liking, 6 to 8 hours.

5 Strain the stock into mason jars and let it cool completely. Store the stock in the refrigerator and let it chill overnight.

6 The next day, remove the layer of fat from the stock. Use as desired, store in the refrigerator for up to 5 days, or in the freezer for up to 1 month.

Sweet Potato Gnocchi

Yield: 6 to 8 Servings
Active Time: 25 Minutes
Total Time: 2 Hours

When sweet potatoes become plentiful in the fall, I take full advantage at my restaurants, incorporating their roasted flesh in a number of preparations. One of the very best ways to utilize it is in a gnocchi, creating the pillowy dumplings you're no doubt familiar with, and supplying a vibrant color that looks intriguing on the plate.

4 lbs. sweet potatoes

¾ cup ricotta cheese

3 egg yolks

1 tablespoon sliced fresh chives

1 tablespoon finely chopped fresh parsley

2 teaspoons fine sea salt, plus more to taste

2 cups all-purpose flour, plus more as needed

1 cup semolina flour

Extra-virgin olive oil, as needed

1 Preheat the oven to 400°F. Wash the sweet potatoes, place them on a parchment-lined baking sheet, and use a knife to poke several holes in their tops. Place in the oven and cook until they are soft all the way through, 45 minutes to 1 hour.

2 Remove the sweet potatoes from the oven, slice them open, and let them cool completely.

3 Scrape the cooled sweet potato flesh into a mixing bowl until you have about 2 cups and mash until it is smooth. Add the ricotta, egg yolks, chives, parsley, and salt, and stir until thoroughly combined.

4 Add the flours 1 cup at a time and work the mixture with your hands until they have been incorporated. When touched, the dough should hold its shape and not stick to your hand. If it is too moist, add more all-purpose flour until the proper consistency has been achieved.

5 Transfer the dough to a flour-dusted work surface and cut it into 10 even pieces. Roll each piece into a long rope and cut the ropes into ¾-inch pieces. Use a fork to roll the gnocchi into the classic shape and place the shaped dumplings on a lightly floured baking sheet.

6 Bring water to a boil in a large pot. Working in small batches, add salt and the gnocchi and stir to keep them from sticking to the bottom. The gnocchi will eventually float to the surface. Cook for 1 more minute, remove them with a pasta fork, and transfer to a bowl.

7 Drizzle a little bit of olive oil over the gnocchi to prevent them from sticking and either serve with your favorite sauce or sauté them in a bit of sage-infused butter.

Sweet Potato Gnocchi, see page 215

Yield: 15 Rolls

Active Time: 30 Minutes

Total Time: 3 Hours and 30 Minutes

Banana & Pecan Cinnamon Rolls

For the Dough

½ cup warm water (105°F)

½ cup crème fraîche

¼ cup sugar

½ cup unsalted butter, softened, plus more as needed

2 teaspoons active dry yeast

2 eggs

3⅔ cups all-purpose flour, plus more as needed

1 ripe banana

For the Filling

1 cup unsalted butter, softened

1½ cups sugar

2 tablespoons cinnamon

1 teaspoon nutmeg

2 teaspoons pure vanilla extract

1 cup toasted pecans, crushed

1 cup raisins

2 ripe bananas, chopped

For the Glaze

4 tablespoons unsalted butter, softened

1⅓ cups confectioners' sugar

¼ cup hot water

When my wife and I owned a bakery, this was one of my favorite pastries that she made. I would often indulge myself with one that was still warm from the oven as I started the lengthy process of mixing, proofing, and baking bread. The crème fraîche is key here, adding creaminess and a tangy element that balances out all the sweetness.

1 To prepare the dough, place all of the ingredients in the work bowl of a stand mixer fitted with the dough hook and mix on low speed until the mixture comes together as a dough. Raise the speed to medium and mix the dough until it is smooth, about 3 minutes. Coat a large bowl with butter, place the dough in it, and cover it with plastic wrap. Place the bowl in a naturally warm spot and let the dough rise until it has doubled in size, about 1 hour.

2 To begin preparations for the filling, place the butter, sugar, cinnamon, nutmeg, and vanilla in a mixing bowl and stir until combined. Set the mixture aside.

3 Place the dough on a flour-dusted work surface and roll it into a 20 x 11–inch rectangle that is about ¼ inch thick.

4 Spread the filling over the dough and then sprinkle the pecans, raisins, and bananas on top. Working from a long side, roll the dough up into a tight log. Using a sharp knife, cut the log into 15 evenly sized pieces.

5 Coat a 15 x 12–inch baking pan with butter and place the rolls in it, leaving about ¾ inch between them. Place the rolls in a naturally warm spot and let them rise until they have doubled in size.

6 Preheat the oven to 350°F.

7 Place the rolls in the oven and bake until they are golden brown, 30 to 40 minutes.

8 While the rolls are in the oven, prepare the glaze. Place the butter and confectioners' sugar in a mixing bowl and stir to combine. While whisking continually, slowly stream in the hot water until the glaze has the desired consistency.

9 Remove the rolls from the oven and drizzle the glaze over the top. Let the rolls cool slightly before serving.

Winter

The winter may mark the end of the growing season, but it is still filled with life, and reasons to celebrate. It is a time to revel in the hard work of the preceding months, to make use of what you have stored up, to crack open a jar of canned tomatoes and remind yourself of the warmth and lightness you knew, and will know again. Winter is a time to gather with your loved ones and enjoy those rich dishes that would have seemed preposterous a month ago, but are now exactly what the moment calls for.

Yield: 4 to 6 Biscuits
Active Time: 20 Minutes
Total Time: 1 Hour

A big piece of being a restaurateur is finding ways to reduce waste and repurpose as many things as you can. Rendered bacon fat is great for sautéing vegetables, but it is also great to bake with, adding a richness that not even butter can approach.

Bacon Fat Biscuits

2 cups all-purpose flour, plus more as needed

2½ teaspoons baking powder

1 tablespoon sugar

1 teaspoon fine sea salt, plus more for topping

½ cup grated cheddar cheese

¼ teaspoon cayenne pepper

½ teaspoon black pepper

¼ teaspoon paprika

½ cup rendered bacon fat, chilled, plus more as needed

1 cup buttermilk, plus more as needed

1 Preheat the oven to 425°F and line a baking sheet with parchment paper. Place all of the ingredients, except for the bacon fat and buttermilk, in a mixing bowl and stir to combine.

2 Add the bacon fat and work the mixture with a pastry blender until it comes together as a crumbly dough.

3 Add the buttermilk and work the mixture until it comes together as a smooth dough. If the dough is too wet, incorporate a little more flour; if it is too dry, incorporate a little more buttermilk.

4 Place the dough on a flour-dusted work surface and use your hands to flatten it into a rectangle. Fold one short end to the center of the dough. Fold the other short end to the center of the dough. Roll the dough flat and repeat the folds to the center.

5 Roll the dough into a 1-inch-thick rectangle and cut it into 2¾-inch rounds.

6 Place the biscuits on the baking sheet, place them in the oven, and bake until the tops start to brown, about 12 minutes.

7 Remove the biscuits from the oven and transfer them to a wire rack to cool slightly.

8 Place some bacon fat in a skillet and warm it over medium heat. Brush the tops of the biscuits with the warmed bacon fat, sprinkle salt over them, and serve.

Yield: 4 Servings
Active Time: 30 Minutes
Total Time: 45 Minutes

Brussels sprouts are something of a controversial ingredient, as some love them, and others positively hate them. I would argue that many in that latter group just haven't had them prepared correctly yet. This recipe is certain to correct that, as frying them provides a great texture, while the acidic vinaigrette adds a brightness that ties everything together.

Crispy Brussels Sprouts

with Maple & Cider Vinaigrette

For the Brussels Sprouts

½ cup diced pancetta

Canola oil, as needed

1 lb. Brussels sprouts, trimmed and halved

½ cup toasted pistachios

Salt and pepper, to taste

½ cup goat cheese, crumbled

1 apple, cored and sliced

For the Vinaigrette

2 tablespoons apple cider vinegar

2 tablespoons apple cider

1 tablespoon maple syrup

1 teaspoon fine sea salt, plus more to taste

1½ teaspoons Dijon mustard

Black pepper, to taste

¾ cup canola oil

1 Place the pancetta in a large skillet and cook it over medium heat until its fat has rendered and it is golden brown, 4 to 6 minutes. Remove the pancetta from the pan and set it aside.

2 Add canola oil to a Dutch oven until it is about 2 inches deep and warm it to 350°F.

3 To prepare the vinaigrette, place all of the ingredients, except for the canola oil, in a small mixing bowl and whisk to combine. While whisking continually, add the canola oil until it has emulsified. Season the vinaigrette with salt and pepper and set it aside.

4 Gently slip the Brussels sprouts into the hot oil and fry until they are crispy and golden brown, 6 to 8 minutes.

5 Transfer the fried Brussels sprouts to a paper towel–lined plate and let them drain.

6 Place the Brussels sprouts in a bowl, add the vinaigrette, pancetta, and pistachios, season with salt and pepper, and toss to combine.

7 Top with the goat cheese and apples and serve.

Yield: 4 to 6 Servings
Active Time: 25 Minutes
Total Time: 1 Hour

I first encountered this comforting vegetarian dish on a visit to my parents' house during a time when my mother was testing out new dishes. After asking for a reasonable serving initially, I found myself going back for seconds and thirds. This version is similar, though I've incorporated Epis to put my own spin on it.

Chickpea Curry

2 tablespoons coconut oil

2 teaspoons curry powder

2 teaspoons adobo seasoning

1 teaspoon allspice

1 tablespoon Epis (see page 104)

3 garlic cloves, minced

1 large onion, diced

2 scallions, trimmed and chopped

Salt, to taste

1 cup diced tomatoes

1 cup diced sweet potato

1 cup diced butternut squash

2 (14 oz.) cans of coconut milk

6 whole cloves

1 habanero chile pepper

3 sprigs of fresh thyme, tied together with kitchen twine

4 cups cooked chickpeas

1 large red bell pepper, stem and seeds removed, diced

White rice, cooked, for serving

1 Place the coconut oil in a medium saucepan and warm it over medium heat. Add the curry powder, adobo, and allspice and toast until fragrant, about 1 minute.

2 Add the Epis, garlic, onion, and scallions, season with salt, and cook, stirring frequently, until the onion is translucent, about 3 minutes.

3 Add the tomatoes, sweet potato, squash, and coconut milk and bring to a simmer. Taste and adjust the seasoning as necessary.

4 Insert the cloves into the habanero. Add it and the thyme to the pan, cover it, and reduce the heat to medium-low. Cook until the curry thickens and the sweet potato and squash are just about fork-tender, about 20 minutes.

5 Stir in the chickpeas and bell pepper and cook until the flavor develops to your liking, 10 to 15 minutes.

6 Remove the thyme and habanero, discard them, and serve the curry over rice.

Yield: 12 to 15 Cupcakes
Active Time: 10 Minutes
Total Time: 1 Hour

When you're assigned dessert duty for a get-together, don't get stressed out—just turn to this simple recipe, which can be prepared well ahead of time and provide the bit of decadence that everyone wants at the end of a winter day.

Chocolate Cupcakes
with Chocolate Buttercream

1 cup all-purpose flour

1 cup sugar

⅓ cup cocoa powder

½ teaspoon baking soda

½ teaspoon baking powder

½ teaspoon fine sea salt

1 egg

½ cup buttermilk

½ cup canola oil

1 teaspoon pure vanilla extract

½ cup hot water

Chocolate Buttercream
(see page 230)

1 Preheat the oven to 300°F and line the wells of a cupcake pan with paper liners.

2 Place the flour, sugar, cocoa powder, baking soda, baking powder, and salt in a large bowl and whisk to combine. Set the mixture aside.

3 Place the egg, buttermilk, canola oil, and vanilla in a separate bowl and whisk to combine.

4 Add the wet mixture to the dry mixture and stir until it comes together as a smooth batter.

5 Stir the hot water into the batter. The batter should be thin.

6 Fill the cupcake liners halfway with the batter. Place the cupcakes in the oven and bake until a cake tester inserted into their centers comes out clean, 15 to 18 minutes. Remove the cupcakes from the oven, transfer them to a wire rack, and let them cool completely.

7 Frost the cupcakes with the buttercream and enjoy.

A rich and luscious frosting that is capable of covering every cake and cupcake that comes out of your oven.

Chocolate Buttercream

1 cup dark chocolate chips

5 egg whites

1 cup sugar

1 tablespoon cocoa powder

Pinch of fine sea salt

1 teaspoon pure vanilla extract

1 lb. unsalted butter, softened and chopped

1 Place the chocolate chips in a heatproof bowl. Bring a few inches of water to a simmer in a medium saucepan, place the bowl over it, and stir until the chocolate is melted. Remove the chocolate from heat and let it cool slightly.

2 Bring the water back to a simmer. Place the egg whites, sugar, cocoa powder, and salt in a separate heatproof bowl. Place it over the water and whisk until the sugar has dissolved. Transfer the mixture to the work bowl of a stand mixer fitted with the whisk attachment and whip until the mixture holds stiff peaks.

3 Add the vanilla and whip to incorporate. With the mixer running, gradually add the butter until it has been incorporated.

4 Add the chocolate, whip to incorporate, and use the frosting immediately or store it in the refrigerator.

This is as good in your morning coffee as it is in cocktails.

Coconut Syrup

1 cup coconut water

2 cups sugar

1 Place the coconut water in a small saucepan and bring to a boil.

2 Add the sugar and stir until the sugar has dissolved.

3 Remove the pan from heat and let the syrup cool completely before using or storing in the refrigerator.

Yield: 1 Drink
Active Time: 5 Minutes
Total Time: 5 Minutes

Whiskey and ginger is a simple, classic, and accessible cocktail that becomes appealing when the temperatures drop. This is a slightly elevated version that I came up with after encountering the The Bitter Truth's Creole Bitters, which are very clove forward. Between that and the bright red hue supplied by the hibiscus, this is a great serve to break out at your holiday parties.

Holiday Season

1 orange wedge

2 oz. whiskey

4 dashes The Bitter Truth Creole Bitters

½ oz. Coconut Syrup (see page 231)

2 oz. iced hibiscus tea

Ginger beer, to top

1 orange wheel, for garnish

1 Luxardo maraschino cherry, for garnish

1 Fill a highball glass with ice and set it aside.

2 Place the orange wedge in a cocktail shaker and muddle it. Add the whiskey, bitters, syrup, and hibiscus tea, fill the shaker halfway with ice, and shake vigorously for 15 minutes.

3 Strain the drink into the highball glass and top with ginger beer.

4 Garnish with the orange wheel and maraschino cherry and enjoy.

Between my wife being a pastry chef, and my own love for baking bread, it made sense for us to open a bakery together. And one of the best treats to come out of that endeavor was these scones, which are irresistibly tart and sweet enough to seem like a treat. Another strength is that they freeze well, so you can make a large batch and know that you have the beginnings of a solid Sunday brunch in reserve.

Cranberry & Orange Scones

3 cups all-purpose flour, plus more as needed

¾ cup sugar

1¼ tablespoons baking powder

1 teaspoon fine sea salt

1 tablespoon orange zest

¾ cup unsalted butter, frozen and grated

¾ cup heavy cream, plus more as needed

2 medium eggs

1 teaspoon pure vanilla extract

¾ cup frozen cranberries, chopped

1 cup confectioners' sugar

6 tablespoons fresh orange juice

1 Line a baking sheet with parchment paper. Place the flour, sugar, baking powder, salt, and orange zest in a large mixing bowl and whisk to combine. Add the butter and work the mixture with your hands until it comes together in pea-sized clumps. Place the bowl in the freezer.

2 Place the cream, eggs, and vanilla in a mixing bowl and whisk to combine. Remove the flour mixture from the freezer, drizzle the egg mixture over it, add the cranberries, and work the mixture until it comes together as a wet dough.

3 Divide the dough into a dozen ½-cup portions. Gently form them into rounds and place them on the baking sheet. Chill the scones in the refrigerator for 20 to 30 minutes.

4 Preheat the oven to 375°F.

5 Brush the scones with heavy cream. Place them in the oven and bake until they are golden brown at the edges and lightly brown on top, 20 to 25 minutes.

6 Remove the scones from the oven, transfer them to a wire rack, and let them cool.

7 Place the confectioners' sugar and orange juice in a bowl and whisk until combined.

8 Drizzle the glaze over the scones and let it set before serving.

Yield: 12 to 15 Pate
Active Time: 30 Minutes
Total Time: 1 Hour and 30 Minutes

Pate is seasoned meat—most commonly ground beef, chicken, or smoked herring—that is encased in a buttery and flaky pastry. These are a great appetizer any time of day, and would work particularly well as part of a brunch spread on a snowy day.

Beef Pate

1 lb. ground beef (85 percent lean recommended)

1½ tablespoons Epis (see page 104)

½ teaspoon sazon

½ teaspoon adobo seasoning

1 teaspoon garlic powder

2 teaspoons fresh lime juice

½ chicken bouillon cube

2 teaspoons soy sauce

¾ cup water

¼ cup diced red bell pepper

¼ cup diced green bell pepper

½ cup diced onion

2 eggs

2 teaspoons canola oil

Quick Pastry Dough (see page 54)

All-purpose flour, as needed

1 Place the ground beef, Epis, sazon, adobo, garlic powder, lime juice, and bouillon cube in a large skillet and cook over medium-high heat for 5 minutes, breaking the ground beef up with a wooden spoon.

2 Add the soy sauce and water and cook until the liquid has just about evaporated and the ground beef is cooked through.

3 Add the peppers and onion and cook until the onion is translucent and the peppers are tender, about 5 minutes.

4 Remove the pan from heat and let the mixture cool completely.

5 Preheat the oven to 350°F and line a baking sheet with parchment paper. Place the eggs and canola oil in a bowl and whisk to combine. Set the mixture aside.

6 Place the sheets of pastry dough on a flour-dusted work surface and roll them out until they are ¼ inch thick. Cut the dough into evenly sized squares and place about 1½ tablespoons of the filling on one side of each square, making sure to leave a ½-inch border.

7 Brush the edges of the squares with the egg mixture, fold the puff pastry over the filling, and crimp the edge with a fork to seal.

8 Place the pate on the baking sheet, brush the tops with the egg mixture, and place them in the oven.

9 Bake until the pate are golden brown, 20 to 25 minutes. Remove them from the oven and let them cool slightly before serving.

Harissa is a spicy chile paste that is commonly used to flavor sauces, soups, and stews, but the first time I encountered it was at a restaurant I worked at early on in my career, where it seasoned the house-made lamb sausage. Take a cue from that preparation and use it as a marinade for meat, in addition to its more common uses.

Harissa

1 head of garlic, halved at the equator

2 tablespoons extra-virgin olive oil

2 bell peppers

2 tablespoons coriander seeds

6 chiles de àrbol

3 pasilla chile peppers

2 shallots, halved

2 teaspoons kosher salt

1 Preheat the oven to 400°F. Place the garlic in a piece of aluminum foil, drizzle half of the olive oil over it, and seal the foil closed.

2 Place the garlic on a baking sheet with the bell peppers and place it in the oven. Roast until the garlic is very tender and the peppers are charred all over. Remove them from the oven and let them cool.

3 While the garlic and peppers are cooling, place the coriander seeds in a dry skillet and toast them over medium heat, shaking the pan frequently. Transfer the coriander seeds to a blender along with the remaining ingredients, including the remaining olive oil.

4 Squeeze the roasted garlic cloves into the blender. Remove the skin, seeds, and stems from the roasted peppers and place the flesh in the blender.

5 Puree until the harissa paste has the desired texture and use immediately or store it in the refrigerator.

Making pasta from scratch can be intimidating, but, as with most things, once you make it a few times, you start to understand how the dough should feel and how you should be handling it. This is a versatile dough that can be used for filled pastas like ravioli or cut into silky strands of tagliatelle.

Homemade Pasta Dough

1 cup all-purpose flour, plus more as needed

7 egg yolks

1 teaspoon extra-virgin olive oil

Pinch of fine sea salt

1 Place the flour on the counter in a mound and make a large well in the center. Place the egg yolks in the well, add the olive oil and salt, and use a fork to gradually incorporate the flour into the egg yolk mixture.

2 Work the mixture with your hands until it comes together as a smooth dough. Form the dough into a ball, cover it with plastic wrap, and let it rest for 30 minutes.

3 Place the dough on a flour-dusted work surface and roll it out until it is thin enough to fit through a pasta maker on its widest setting.

4 Run the dough through the pasta maker until it is thin enough to see your hand through it. Dust the dough with flour and reduce the pasta machine to a thinner setting with each pass.

5 Cut the dough into the desired shapes and keep in mind that fresh pasta will cook 3 to 4 times as fast as dried pasta.

Yield: 16 Cups
Active Time: 45 Minutes
Total Time: 2 Hours

Incorporating mushrooms in a Bolognese is not traditional, but I find that their earthiness is a nice—and necessary—counter to the sweetness supplied by the carrots and tomatoes. This is a great dish to whip up in the days leading up to the holidays, as it is a largely hands-off preparation that will allow for much discussion with friends and family who are visiting.

Bolognese Sauce

2 tablespoons extra-virgin olive oil

1 lb. ground beef

Salt and pepper, to taste

¼ lb. bacon, chopped

1 onion, diced

1 carrot, peeled and diced

3 celery stalks, diced

½ cup diced portabella mushrooms

2 garlic cloves, minced

½ cup red wine

6 cups crushed tomatoes

¼ cup fresh basil, sliced thin

2 tablespoons finely chopped fresh parsley

Homemade Pasta Dough (see page 241), cooked, for serving

1 Place the olive oil in a cast-iron Dutch oven and warm it over medium heat. Add the ground beef, season the mixture with salt and pepper, and cook, breaking the ground beef up with a wooden spoon as it browns, until it is cooked through, about 8 minutes.

2 Remove the ground beef from the pot and set it aside. Add the bacon, reduce the heat to medium-low, and cook the bacon until its fat renders and it is crispy, 6 to 8 minutes.

3 Add the onion, carrot, celery, mushrooms, and garlic, season the mixture with salt and pepper, and cook, stirring frequently, until the onion is translucent, about 3 minutes.

4 Raise the heat to high and deglaze the pan with the wine, scraping up any browned bits from the bottom of the pan.

5 Add the tomatoes, return the ground beef, and reduce the heat to medium-low. Season the sauce with salt and pepper and cook the sauce until the flavor has developed to your liking, about 1½ hours.

6 Stir in the basil and parsley and taste the sauce. Adjust the seasoning as necessary and serve it over the pasta.

Yield: 24 Madeleines
Active Time: 20 Minutes
Total Time: 3 Hours

I have been lucky to spend time in France, and the madeleine is one symbol of that time, as I fell in love with it during my visit. Somewhere between a cake and a cookie, these treats also hold a special place in my heart because my daughter's name is Madeleine. In the month leading up to her birth, I served these at the restaurant as a mignardise (a small confection), giving everyone a subtle, playful hint of what was to come.

Madeleines

4 tablespoons unsalted butter, plus more as needed

⅔ cup brown sugar

2 eggs

1 tablespoon grated fresh ginger

1 teaspoon pure vanilla extract

¾ teaspoon molasses

¼ cup milk

¼ cup all-purpose flour

½ cup cake flour

¼ teaspoon baking powder

1 teaspoon fine sea salt

⅛ teaspoon ground cloves

¼ teaspoon freshly grated nutmeg

1 teaspoon cinnamon

Confectioners' sugar, for topping

1 Place the butter in a small saucepan and melt it over medium heat. Continue cooking the butter until it just starts to brown and give off a nutty aroma. Pour the brown butter into a bowl and let it cool completely.

2 Place the brown sugar and brown butter in the work bowl of a stand mixer fitted with the whisk attachment and whip on high until the mixture is light and frothy.

3 Reduce the speed to medium and incorporate the eggs one at a time, scraping down the work bowl as needed. Add the ginger, vanilla, molasses, and milk and whip until they are incorporated.

4 Sift the flours and baking powder into a separate bowl. Add the salt, cloves, nutmeg, and cinnamon and stir to combine.

5 With the mixer running, gradually add the dry mixture to the work bowl until it comes together as a dough. Form the dough into a ball, cover it with plastic wrap, and chill it in the refrigerator for 2 hours.

6 Preheat the oven to 375°F.

7 Using a pastry brush, coat each shell in a madeleine pan with butter. Place the madeleine pan in the freezer and chill for 10 minutes.

8 Remove the pan from the freezer and fill each shell two-thirds of the way with dough.

9 Place the madeleines in the oven and bake until they are golden brown and a cake tester inserted into their centers comes out clean, about 12 minutes.

10 Remove the madeleines from the oven, remove them from the pan, and place them on a wire rack. Serve warm or at room temperature, dusting them with confectioners' sugar before serving.

Thyme has a hearty, foresty flavor that was made to incorporate into a winter warmer. As the winter is also the time when citrus is at its best, this cocktail is a must when the light starts to dwindle.

Orange Thyme

2 oz. bourbon

2 oz blood orange juice

1 oz. Honey & Thyme Syrup (see page 249)

Seltzer, to top

1 blood orange wheel, for garnish

1 sprig of fresh thyme, for garnish

1 Fill a highball glass with ice and set it aside.

2 Place the bourbon, juice, and syrup in a cocktail shaker, fill it halfway with ice, and shake vigorously for 15 seconds.

3 Strain the drink over ice and top with seltzer.

4 Garnish the cocktail with the blood orange wheel and thyme and enjoy.

Yield: ¾ Cup
Active Time: 10 Minutes
Total Time: 30 Minutes

Honey is a great ingredient to incorporate into a cocktail syrup, as its round, floral sweetness complements the citrus that is present in most drinks.

Honey & Thyme Syrup

¼ cup water

½ cup honey

2 sprigs of fresh thyme

1 Place the water in a small saucepan and bring it to a boil.

2 Add the honey and thyme and stir until the honey has liquefied.

3 Remove the pan from heat and let the syrup steep until it has cooled completely.

4 Strain the syrup before using or storing in the refrigerator.

Yield: 18 Rolls
Active Time: 30 Minutes
Total Time: 2 Hours

I knew these rolls were going to be a hit at the bakery the second that I got the recipe pinned down. The proofing times will vary depending on the ambient temperatures in your home, but they are relatively short for a bread, particularly one so buttery and fluffy.

Parker House Rolls

½ cup lukewarm water (90°F)

¾ teaspoon active dry yeast

2½ tablespoons sugar

2 cups all-purpose flour, plus more as needed

¾ teaspoon fine sea salt

2 eggs

4 tablespoons unsalted butter, softened, plus more as needed

1 teaspoon milk

1 Place the water, yeast, and sugar in the work bowl of a stand mixer fitted with the dough hook, gently stir, and let the mixture sit until it starts to foam, about 10 minutes.

2 Add the flour, salt, 1 egg, and the butter and mix on low speed until combined. Raise the speed to high and mix until the mixture comes together as a smooth, elastic dough.

3 Coat a large bowl with butter, place the dough in it, and cover it with plastic wrap. Let the dough rise in a naturally warm spot until it has doubled in size, about 30 minutes.

4 Coat three small cast-iron pans with nonstick cooking spray. Place the dough on a flour-dusted work surface and cut it into 18 pieces (they should each weigh around 1¼ oz.). Roll the pieces into tight balls and place them in the pans. Cover the pans with kitchen towels and let the rolls rise in a naturally warm spot until they have doubled in size and are touching each other, about 30 minutes.

5 Preheat the oven to 325°F. Place the milk and remaining egg in a bowl and whisk to combine. Brush the tops of the rolls with the egg wash and place them in the oven.

6 Bake until the rolls are golden brown, 25 to 30 minutes. Remove the rolls from the oven and let them cool slightly before serving.

Yield: 2 Servings
Active Time: 25 Minutes
Total Time: 3 Hours

Save this one for those moments when you have some time before you'll be called on to serve the dish, but are short on attention to devote to preparing something memorable, as the more time you have to let the chicken marinate in the bold Harissa, the better. The Pickled Red Onion is a nice touch here, providing an acidic bite that cuts beautifully against the rich, deep flavors of the main.

Roasted Chicken Breast
with Harissa & Pickled Red Onion

1 lb. skin-on boneless chicken breasts

½ cup Harissa (see page 238)

1½ tablespoons canola oil

Salt and pepper, to taste

2 tablespoons extra-virgin olive oil

2 tablespoons minced shallot

1 garlic clove, minced

¼ cup Roasted Chicken Stock (see page 214)

2 teaspoons fresh lime juice

3 tablespoons unsalted butter, cubed

Pickled Red Onion (see page 120), for garnish

1 Rub the chicken breasts with 2 tablespoons of the Harissa. Place them in a bowl and let them marinate in the refrigerator for 2 hours.

2 Preheat the oven to 350°F.

3 Place the canola oil in a large cast-iron skillet and warm it over medium-high heat. Season the chicken with salt and pepper and place it in the pan, skin side down. Place the chicken in the oven and roast until the skin is crispy, 8 to 10 minutes.

4 Turn the chicken over and roast until the internal temperature is 165°F, 10 to 15 minutes.

5 While the chicken is in the oven, place the olive oil in a large skillet and warm it over medium heat. Add the shallot and garlic and cook, stirring frequently, until the shallot is translucent, about 3 minutes.

6 Stir in the remaining Harissa, stock, and lime juice and bring to a boil. Reduce the heat, gradually add the butter, and whisk to emulsify.

7 Remove the pan from heat, taste the sauce, and adjust the seasoning as necessary. Set the sauce aside.

8 Remove the chicken from the oven and let it rest for 5 minutes.

9 Ladle the sauce onto the serving plates. Slice the chicken and place it on top of the sauce. Garnish with Pickled Red Onion and enjoy.

Yield: 2 Servings

Active Time: 20 Minutes

Total Time: 20 Minutes

This sandwich was born out of a desire to come up with a spin on the classic Reuben, with the sun-dried tomato spread and Pickled Red Cabbage combining to produce a brighter and lighter sandwich that still satisfies.

Pastrami Sandwiches

with Sun-Dried Tomato Mayo & Pickled Red Cabbage

For the Mayo

½ cup chopped sun-dried tomatoes in olive oil

½ cup mayonnaise

1½ teaspoons whole-grain mustard

1 tablespoon chopped fresh parsley

1 tablespoon sliced scallions

1 tablespoon relish

1½ teaspoons horseradish

½ teaspoon Worcestershire sauce

½ teaspoon chopped garlic

1 teaspoon fine sea salt

½ teaspoon black pepper

For the Sandwiches

4 slices of Potato Bread (see page 191)

4 slices of cheddar cheese

7 oz. Pastrami (see page 257), sliced

½ cup Pickled Red Cabbage (see page 188)

1 red onion, sliced

1 Preheat a panini press.

2 To prepare the mayo, place all of the ingredients in a bowl and stir until well combined.

3 To prepare the sandwiches, spread some of the mayo on each slice of bread. Top with the cheese, Pastrami, cabbage, and onion and assemble the sandwiches.

4 Place the sandwiches in the panini press and toast until they are golden brown on each side and the cheese has melted. Serve immediately.

NOTE: If you don't have a panini press, don't worry. Simply place 1 tablespoon of olive oil in a large skillet and warm it over medium heat. Place a sandwich in the pan, place a cast-iron skillet on top so it is pressing down on the sandwich, and cook until golden brown. Turn the sandwich over and repeat.

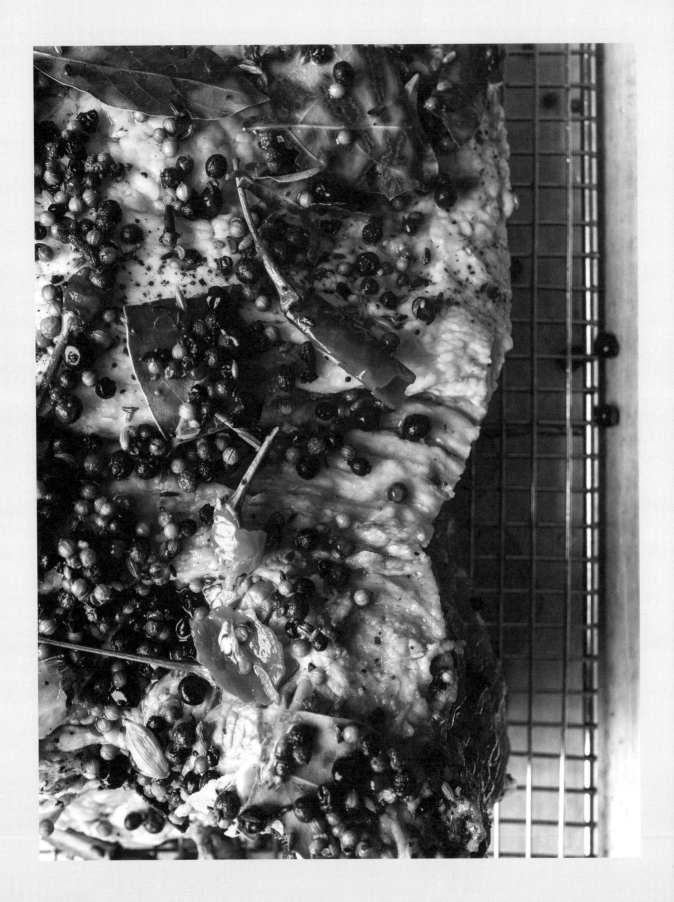

Pastrami

Yield: 10 to 12 Servings
Active Time: 1 Hour
Total Time: 5 Days

Making pastrami at home is much simpler than you think, and the end result is far superior to anything you could find at your local supermarket. Although a bit of patience is required, as the preparation takes 5 days, you will not be disappointed with the end result. If the brisket is too large to remain submerged in the brine, it may need to be cut in half. Any leftovers can be wrapped tightly in plastic and stored in the fridge for up to a week.

For the Brine

12 cups water

1 cup kosher salt

½ cup sugar

¼ cup brown sugar

¼ teaspoon curing salt

¼ cup black peppercorns

2 tablespoons fennel seeds

2 tablespoons coriander seeds

1 tablespoon caraway seeds

1½ teaspoons red pepper flakes

10 garlic cloves, crushed

24 cups ice

For the Pastrami

3 to 4 lb. beef brisket, trimmed of excess fat

¼ cup coriander seeds

¼ cup black peppercorns

2 tablespoons fennel seeds

1 To begin preparations for the brine, place all of the ingredients, except for the ice, in a stockpot and bring to a boil, stirring to dissolve the salt and sugars.

2 Place the ice in a container large enough to fit the brine and brisket, but small enough to fit in the refrigerator. Pour the mixture in the stockpot over the ice and let the brine cool completely.

3 To begin preparations for the pastrami, place the brisket in the brine and make sure it is fully submerged. Cover the container and let the brisket brine in the refrigerator for 5 days.

4 Preheat the oven to 300°F. Remove the brisket from the brine and pat it dry.

5 Using a mortar and pestle or a spice grinder, coarsely grind the coriander seeds, peppercorns, and fennel seeds. Rub the mixture over the brisket and wrap it tightly with aluminum foil.

6 Place the brisket on a baking sheet and place it in the oven.

7 Cook until the brisket's interior temperature is 200°F, 4 to 5 hours.

8 Remove the brisket from the oven and let it rest for 30 minutes

9 Cut the pastrami into ¼-inch-thick slices and enjoy as is or on a sandwich.

Yield: 1 Cake
Active Time: 20 Minutes
Total Time: 1 Hour and 30 Minutes

One of my all-time favorite desserts is a classic Haitian pineapple upside-down cake, because it seems like little more than your standard buttery, moist pound cake, but it features warming spice and a subtle hint of citrus from the lime zest. There are many different family recipes out there, but this topping is the one that you will encounter the most often.

Pineapple Upside-Down Cake

¾ cup unsalted butter, plus more as needed

¼ cup brown sugar

4 to 6 pineapple rings, drained

4 to 6 cocktail cherries, stems removed

¼ cup raisins

1¾ cups all-purpose flour

½ teaspoon kosher salt

1½ teaspoons freshly grated nutmeg

1 tablespoon baking powder

1⅛ cups sugar

2 eggs

1 teaspoon lime zest

1 teaspoon pure vanilla extract

½ teaspoon almond extract

1 tablespoon Haitian rum

¾ cup pineapple juice

1 Preheat the oven to 325°F and position a rack in the center. Coat the bottom and sides of a round 9-inch cake pan generously with butter. Sprinkle the brown sugar over the bottom of the pan, cover with the pineapple rings, and place a cherry in the center of each pineapple ring. Fill every empty space between the pineapple rings with raisins and set the pan aside.

2 Place the flour, salt, nutmeg, and baking powder in a mixing bowl, whisk to combine, and set the mixture aside.

3 Place the butter and sugar in the work bowl of a stand mixer fitted with the whisk attachment and whip on high until the mixture is creamy and pale. Scrape down the work bowl and whip on high for 1 minute.

4 Add the eggs and whip until incorporated.

5 Add the lime zest, vanilla, almond extract, rum, and pineapple juice and whip until well combined, scraping down the work bowl as needed. The mix will separate slightly, but don't worry—the next step will bring it together again.

6 Add the flour mixture and whip until the mixture just comes together as a smooth batter, taking care not to overwork the mixture.

7 Pour the batter into the pan and tap it on the counter to distribute the batter evenly and remove any air bubbles.

8 Place the cake in the oven and bake for 30 minutes.

9 Turn the pan 180° and bake until a cake tester inserted into the center of the cake comes out clean, 20 to 30 minutes.

10 Remove the cake from the oven and let it cool for 30 minutes.

11 Place a large plate over the pan and carefully invert the pan so that the cake slides out onto the plate. Let the cake cool completely before slicing and serving.

Parker House Rolls, see page 250

Yield: 4 to 6 Servings
Active Time: 30 Minutes
Total Time: 2 Hours

This is an elaborate-looking salad that is actually very easy to prepare. Sweet, tart, nutty, and earthy, it's a grain-centric salad that is hearty enough to work as a main. You could serve this dish warm, but it is at its best at room temperature.

Toasted Farro Salad

½ cup extra-virgin olive oil

2 cups farro

Salt and pepper, to taste

5 cups water

½ bunch of kale, stems removed, leaves torn

½ cup sunflower seeds

1 large sweet potato, peeled and diced

2 parsnips, trimmed and diced

¼ cup apple cider vinegar

1 teaspoon Dijon mustard

2 tablespoons sliced fresh chives

2 tablespoons chopped fresh parsley

1 tablespoon diced shallot

½ cup dried cranberries

1 Preheat the oven to 400°F. Place 2 tablespoons of the olive oil in a medium saucepan and warm it over medium heat. Add the farro and toast it, shaking the pan occasionally, until it gives off a nutty aroma.

2 Season the farro with salt, add the water, and bring to a boil. Reduce the heat and simmer the farro until it has absorbed the water and is al dente, 25 to 40 minutes. Spread the farro on a baking sheet in an even layer and let it cool completely.

3 Line two baking sheets with parchment paper. Place the kale in a mixing bowl, add 1 tablespoon of the remaining olive oil, and season with salt and pepper. Toss to combine and place the kale on half of one of the baking sheets. Place the sunflower seeds on the other half of the baking sheet.

4 Place the pan in the oven and roast until the kale is crispy and the sunflower seeds are toasted, 8 to 10 minutes. Remove the pan from the oven and set it aside.

5 Place the sweet potato and parsnips in a mixing bowl, add 1 tablespoon of the remaining olive oil, and season with salt and pepper. Toss to combine and place the sweet potato and parsnips on the other baking sheet.

6 Place the pan in the oven and roast until the vegetables are tender, 20 to 30 minutes. Remove the vegetables from the oven and let them cool completely.

7 Place the remaining olive oil, the vinegar, mustard, chives, parsley, and shallot in a bowl, season with salt and pepper, and whisk to combine. Set the vinaigrette aside.

8 Place the farro, roasted vegetables, toasted sunflower seeds, and dried cranberries in a mixing bowl, add the vinaigrette, and toss to combine. Serve immediately.

This tart and zesty condiment is wonderful over roasted meats, and it's also worth keeping in mind if you're putting together a charcuterie board for company.

Cranberry Mostarda

½ cup dried cranberries, chopped

1 teaspoon diced shallot

2 teaspoons whole-grain mustard

1 tablespoon chopped fresh parsley

2 teaspoons sliced fresh chives

1½ tablespoons extra-virgin olive oil

1 teaspoon honey

2 teaspoons sherry vinegar

1 Place all of the ingredients in a small bowl and stir to combine.

2 Taste the mostarda, adjust the seasoning as necessary, and either use immediately or store it in the refrigerator.

Yield: 4 Servings
Active Time: 5 Minutes
Total Time: 15 Minutes

These crispy, earthy veggie chips are great as a side for roasted meats, adding nutrition and texture. They are also great as a snack, and you should feel free to get inventive with the seasonings you use, keeping in mind the other flavors that are on the table.

Kale Chips

½ bunch of kale

3 tablespoons extra-virgin olive oil

Salt and pepper, to taste

1 Preheat the oven to 350°F. Remove the leaves of the kale from the stems and tear the leaves. Place them in a bowl, add the olive oil, and season with salt and pepper. Toss to combine.

2 Place the kale on a baking sheet and place it in the oven. Bake until the kale is crispy, 6 to 8 minutes.

3 Remove the kale chips from the oven and either use immediately or store them in an airtight container.

Yield: 2 Servings
Active Time: 20 Minutes
Total Time: 30 Minutes

High-quality duck can be difficult to source at a standard grocery store, so it's best to find a farm in your area that sells it. Once you do, remember that the key to successfully cooking duck breasts is to score the skin, as it helps the fat render and allows the skin to become crispy.

Roasted Duck Breast
with Cranberry Mostarda & Kale Chips

4 oz. fresh cranberries

2 red apples, cored and chopped

¼ cup sugar

2 teaspoons diced shallot

1 teaspoon apple cider vinegar

2 teaspoons kosher salt, plus more to taste

1 lb. skin-on duck breasts

Black pepper, to taste

1 tablespoon unsalted butter

Cranberry Mostarda (see page 264), for serving

Kale Chips (see page 265), for serving

1 Place the cranberries, apples, sugar, shallot, vinegar, and salt in a small saucepan and cook over medium heat until the cranberries are soft and the mixture has reduced slightly.

2 Strain the mixture, reserving the liquid, and place it in a blender. Puree until smooth, adding the reserved liquid as needed to get the desired consistency. Set the puree aside.

3 Trim any excess fat from the duck and score the skin with a sharp knife. Season the skin side with salt, turn the duck over, and season the flesh side with salt and pepper.

4 Place the duck, skin side down, in a large cast-iron skillet and cook it over medium-low heat until the fat starts to render. Drain all of the fat that collects in the pan and closely monitor the heat so that the skin doesn't get too brown before it has a chance to become crispy.

5 When the duck's skin is crispy, turn it over and cook for 2 minutes. Add the butter and baste the duck until the internal temperature is about 130°F.

6 Remove the duck from the pan and let it rest for a few minutes.

7 Spread some puree over each of the serving plates. Slice the duck, set it atop the puree, and serve with the Cranberry Mostarda and Kale Chips.

These easy-to-prepare and comforting tarts are a godsend on those days when the winter really starts to wear on you.

Vanilla Tarts

For the Cookies

½ cup unsalted butter

1 cup brown sugar

1 cup rolled oats

1½ tablespoons all-purpose flour

½ teaspoon fine sea salt

1 small egg

½ teaspoon pure vanilla extract

For the Meringue

½ cup water

1 cup sugar

4 egg whites

¼ teaspoon cream of tartar

4 Tart Shells (see page 272)

Pastry Cream (see page 273)

1 Preheat the oven to 325°F and line two baking sheets with parchment paper. To begin preparations for the cookies, place the butter and brown sugar in a medium saucepan and melt over medium heat. Add the remaining ingredients and stir until well combined.

2 Form tablespoons of the dough into balls, place them on the baking sheets, and place them in the oven. Bake until they are golden brown and crispy, 5 to 7 minutes. Remove the cookies from the oven and transfer them to a wire rack to cool.

3 To begin preparations for the meringue, place the water and sugar in a small saucepan and bring to a boil, stirring to dissolve the sugar. Continue cooking until the syrup is 240°F.

4 While waiting for the syrup to warm up, place the egg whites and cream of tartar in the work bowl of a stand mixer fitted with the whisk attachment and whip on high until the mixture holds stiff peaks.

5 With the mixer running, slowly stream in the syrup. Whip until the meringue has cooled and holds stiff peaks. Place the meringue in a piping bag fitted with a fluted tip.

6 Fill the Tart Shells with the Pastry Cream and pipe the meringue over the top. Using a kitchen torch, carefully toast the meringue until it is golden brown. Top each tart with the oat cookies and serve.

A good preparation to have at hand all year, as they allow you to either capture what is fresh in a particular season, or soothe what is grating about it.

Tart Shells

1 cup all-purpose flour, plus more as needed

Pinch of fine sea salt

⅛ teaspoon baking powder

¾ tablespoon sugar

6 tablespoons unsalted butter, chilled

1 small egg

1 tablespoon heavy cream

1 Place the flour, salt, baking powder, and sugar in a food processor and pulse until combined. Add the cold butter and pulse until the mixture is a collection of pea-sized crumbs.

2 Add the egg and heavy cream and pulse until the mixture just comes together as a crumbly dough. Form it into a disk, cover it in plastic wrap, and chill it in the refrigerator for 30 minutes.

3 Preheat the oven to 325°F.

4 Coat four miniature tart pans with nonstick cooking spray. Place the dough on a flour-dusted work surface and roll it out into a ¼-inch-thick rectangle. Cut the dough into 3-inch rounds and place them in the miniature tart pans.

5 Place the pans on a baking sheet, place them in the oven, and bake until they are golden brown, 10 to 12 minutes.

6 Remove the tart shells from the oven and let them cool completely.

Yield: 1¼ Cups
Active Time: 20 Minutes
Total Time: 1 Hour

You'll most likely be using this as a filling for tarts, pies, and pastries, but it is so luscious that you could easily serve it on its own.

Pastry Cream

1 cup whole milk

2 tablespoons sugar

Pinch fine sea salt

Seeds of 1 vanilla pod

2 egg yolks

1 tablespoon cornstarch

1 teaspoon all-purpose flour

1½ tablespoons unsalted butter

1 Place the milk, sugar, salt, and vanilla seeds in a small saucepan and bring to a simmer, stirring to dissolve the sugar and salt.

2 Place the egg yolks, cornstarch, and flour in a bowl and whisk to combine.

3 While whisking continually, add half of the warm milk mixture to the egg yolk mixture. Pour the tempered egg yolk mixture into the saucepan and cook, stirring continually, until the custard thickens and reaches about 170°F.

4 Remove the pan from heat and strain the custard into a heatproof bowl. Stir in the butter, place plastic wrap directly on the surface of the custard to prevent a skin from forming, and chill it in the refrigerator until it is completely cool.

The Espresso Martini has been resurfacing everywhere of late, which got me thinking of ways to incorporate coffee into a cocktail. As rum has far more flavor than the vodka that typically features in an Espresso Martini, I'm confident my riff will provide the pick-me-up you and your loved ones want while talking late into the winter night. Also, it's imperative that you use a warm shot of espresso even though it will cool in the shaker, as it will supply the crema you're looking for.

The coffee bean garnish is there for more than just aesthetics, as tradition holds that they represent health, wealth, and happiness.

Wake-Up Call

2 oz. Barbancourt 5-Star rum

½ oz. Caffè Borghetti espresso liqueur

1 oz. freshly brewed espresso

½ oz. Simple Syrup (see page 39)

3 coffee beans, for garnish

1 Chill a coupe in the freezer.

2 Place all of the ingredients, except for the coffee beans, in a cocktail shaker, fill it halfway with ice, and shake vigorously for 15 seconds.

3 Strain into the chilled coupe, garnish with the coffee beans, and enjoy.

Metric Conversions

US Measurement	Approximate Metric Liquid Measurement	Approximate Metric Dry Measurement
1 teaspoon	5 ml	5 g
1 tablespoon or ½ ounce	15 ml	14 g
1 ounce or ⅛ cup	30 ml	29 g
¼ cup or 2 ounces	60 ml	57 g
⅓ cup	80 ml	76 g
½ cup or 4 ounces	120 ml	113 g
⅔ cup	160 ml	151 g
¾ cup or 6 ounces	180 ml	170 g
1 cup or 8 ounces or ½ pint	240 ml	227 g
1½ cups or 12 ounces	350 ml	340 g
2 cups or 1 pint or 16 ounces	475 ml	454 g
3 cups or 1½ pints	700 ml	680 g
4 cups or 2 pints or 1 quart	950 ml	908 g

Index

Acknowledgments

Chris Viaud

Since early on in my time in the industry, I have had an obsession with purchasing cookbooks, using them to educating myself on new and interesting techniques and flavor profiles. My extensive collection now ranges from fine dining and backyard barbeques to breads, pastries, and pastas, but it wasn't until I wrote my first cookbook years ago that I had any idea how much work went into creating each of these books. An immense amount of time, dedication, and sacrifice went into cooking, writing, and photographing the preparations in *Gather*, and it goes without saying that I never could have made it through this process without the support of my amazing friends and family.

To my wife, Emilee—none of what I have been able to accomplish over the years would have been possible without the enormous amount of support you have provided. You have allowed me the opportunity to successfully expand my dining group with multiple restaurant concepts, all while you run your own business, Sweet Treats by Emilee. I am so proud of your passion and the dedication you have for your company, and I'm there to support you always. We've built a beautiful life together and accumulated so many stories along the way—we have much to be proud of. Of course, the biggest pride and joy we share is not a culinary or business success, but our beautiful baby girl, Madeleine Eve.

Maddie, ti elefan mwen an. You bring your mother and I a new sense of purpose, and fuel our desire to be the very best versions of ourselves. All we accomplish in the years to come is to create a better future for you and to ensure we provide you with every opportunity you desire. Thank you both for your patience and unconditional love.

To our pup Oaklee: you have been a blessing. Thank you for the joy you have brought into our lives. I love you all with all my heart!

My brother Phil—you helped make this book a truly captivating piece of art with your incredible eye for photography. You were able to take what I presented on the plate and capture the beauty present in it.

You are an incredible photographer and I'm glad to be able to share your talents alongside mine with this legacy project. I admire your humble nature, and look up to you for who you are and all that you have accomplished. I'm so proud of you, and know you will achieve all that you set out to.

My parents, Yves and Myrlene—thank you for all that you have done for me. I wouldn't be the man I am today without you both by my side, constantly pushing me to pursue my dreams and achieve my goals. You are my number one fans, and with your support I know I can accomplish anything I set my mind to. I appreciate all the words of wisdom that you have shared—they guide each and every major decision I make.

My younger sisters, Kassie and Katie, you are two beautiful young women with extremely bright futures ahead of you and I thank you for always being there when Emilee, Maddie, and I need you. I am truly blessed to have you in my life and I can't thank you enough. I love you both!

To all of the others who hold a special place in my heart, from family and friends to the staff at my restaurants Greenleaf, Ansanm, and Pavilion, the From the Field Catering crew, and my culinary instructors, you all have impacted me greatly—not only my career, but also in the way I carry myself day to day. I thank you for all being there when I needed it. Through your love and support I have been able to push through numerous boundaries and face challenging obstacles, which has strengthened my belief in myself and what I am capable of. I know that with you all behind my back, I will accomplish whatever it is that I may set out to do.

Lastly, I'd like to thank the entire team at Cider Mill Press for the opportunity to produce this cookbook, and for making the process a lot less stressful than it could have been. I appreciate you allowing us to share our story, and we hope to inspire those who read this cookbook to share some of our recipes with their friends and family.

Phil Viaud

Gratitude is the word that comes to mind when I think about this project. I'm grateful for the opportunity to photograph food that has meaning to me and represents part of my childhood. I'm also grateful for the opportunity to do all of this with my brother.

For this book to be the success that it is, however, it took more than the two of us, and I appreciate all of those involved.

Thank you to my wife, Sarah, who is my partner in life! Thank you for showing me how to love with intention. For believing in me, and for supporting me in this endeavor, and everything I do. For being my biggest cheerleader. You bring joy and laughter to my life and you are someone I can always talk to. You are someone I can show all my photos to, the good, the bad, and the ugly (never the funny candids of you). Thank you for challenging me to become a better person, partner, and dog dad to our loving pup, Drake. You are my light and my love!

I'm truly grateful for my family. Thanks to my brother, Chris, for thinking of me and asking me to take part in this cookbook. Your passion, hard work, and creativity shows in everything you do, and I'm proud of all that you have set your sights on and accomplished.

To my mother and father—I'm truly lucky to have parents like the two of you. Thank you for showing me what it means to be a good person, how to work hard to achieve your goals, and for always being there no matter what. I appreciate all you have done in helping shape who I am today.

To my sisters, Kassie and Katie, thank you for the support you've given. I'm grateful to have two amazing sisters with your drive, dedication, and compassion.

Lastly, to my in-laws, Susan and Juan—thank you for your love, support, and guidance.

About the Author

Chris Viaud, a James Beard Award semifinalist in 2022 and a *Top Chef* alumnus, is the chef and owner of Greenleaf and Ansanm, both of which are located in Milford, New Hampshire, and Pavilion, which is in Wolfeboro, New Hampshire. All three restaurants are part of his hospitality company, Northern Comfort Dining Group.

Upon graduating from Johnson & Wales, Chris moved to Boston, where he spent three formative years working his way through the ranks at Deuxave. Since his time in Boston he has been an essential part of multiple restaurant openings in the Greater Boston and New Hampshire areas. Chef Viaud's food is rustic in its approach, yet refined by classic techniques. His passion for seasonal products, most of which are grown locally, serves as a guide when creating menus featuring balanced dishes that incorporate different flavors and textures to entertain the palate.

Chef Viaud has recently begun focusing a lot more time and energy on exploring his Haitian heritage, including finding ways to introduce other communities to the beauty of Haitian cuisine and culture. Believing that every day contains an opportunity to learn something new, he continues to push the boundaries, constantly taking himself out of his comfort zone by exploring new ideas, styles, trends, and concepts.

About Cider Mill Press Book Publishers

Good ideas ripen with time. From seed to harvest, Cider Mill Press brings fine reading, information, and entertainment together between the covers of its creatively crafted books. Our Cider Mill bears fruit twice a year, publishing a new crop of titles each spring and fall.

"Where Good Books Are Ready for Press"
501 Nelson Place
Nashville, Tennessee 37214

cidermillpress.com